*For my strong, beautiful and determined daughter,
Etta. My driving force. I love you.* – SARAH KLYMKIW

*Dedicated to Clare. Who knew how to not shop and
borrow clothes highly effectively from me for most
of her teenage years. You're a pioneer sis. x* – KIM HANKINSON

First published in Great Britain 2020 by Red Shed,
an imprint of Egmont UK Limited
2 Minster Court, London EC3R 7BB
www.egmont.co.uk

Text copyright © Sarah Klymkiw 2020
Inside illustrations copyright © Kim Hankinson 2020
Cover illustrations copyright © Egmont Ltd 2020

Sarah Klymkiw and Kim Hankinson
have asserted their moral rights.

Cover illustrated by Thy Bui.

ISBN 978 7 4052 9565 9
70643/001
Printed in Italy.

A CIP catalogue record for this book
is available from the British Library.

Stay safe online. Any website addresses listed in
this book are correct at the time of going to print.
However, Egmont is not responsible for content
hosted by third parties. Please be aware that
online content can be subject to change and
websites can contain content that is unsuitable
for children. We advise that all children are
supervised when using the internet.

Adult supervision may be required for some
of the activities within the book.

Egmont takes its responsibility to the planet and
its inhabitants very seriously. We aim to use papers
from well-managed forests run by responsible suppliers.

FASHION CONSCIOUS

SARAH KLYMKIW
AND KIM HANKINSON

RED SHED

A Letter from the Author

Behind the scenes of the apparently glossy and glamorous world of fashion there's a machine. The machine is well-oiled and churns out new clothes every second of every minute of every hour of every day. The machine crosses continents and it takes precious natural resources, such as plants, water, oil and animals, and turns them into clothes that we may wear once or twice before being resigned to the back of a cupboard, taken to the charity shop or tossed into the bin.

This is because fashion exists in a world that encourages us to buy. And buy we do. By buying, we keep the wheels of the machine moving. The machine churns out more and more stuff in a world that arguably needs to be producing less.

The fashion machine needs us to continue buying so it can continue, but this is not sustainable. Not if we are to seriously bring down carbon emissions, halt the depletion of precious resources, tackle pollution and waste and improve the lives of the people who make our clothes.

It's my hope that after reading this book you will continue to love clothes as much as I do, but with open eyes to the impact that our clothing choices have on people and our planet. I hope that you will feel empowered to demand answers to questions and take action. We have the power to collectively change the world with a change of clothes.

Sarah Klymkiw

CONTENTS

FOLLOWER OF FASHION?

Clothes are a basic necessity that protect us from the elements, but they also help us to engage with the world around us. They allow us to express ourselves and interact with other people without uttering so much as a word. They're mostly a personal choice and can be a crucial part of shaping our own identity. Clothes are one of the first things we see when we meet someone new, and they influence our first impressions of them.

Humans have a long tradition of decorating their bodies for rituals and to show their social status. The changing trends in the way that we use clothes to decorate our bodies are collectively known as fashion.

IT'S ARGUED THAT FASHION SATISFIES AN INNATE HUMAN DESIRE FOR CHANGE.

In the modern world, there is a fashion system that is responsible for setting trends and changing tastes. It is a cycle that is continuously changing, and to keep up with fashion trends can sometimes feel unachievable. However, you can still love clothes and develop your own sense of style without slavishly following trends. Style is how you adapt clothes and fashion trends to make your own personal statement. Style is timeless and won't date. You can dip your toes in and out of what's hot and what's not and still enjoy fashion without buying more clothes. Besides, who wants to look the same as everyone else?

Clothes tell their own story . . .

Clothes are a form of storytelling. They have a built-in story behind them, and new stories are created when we wear them. People are part of that story because fashion is made by people for people. The hands of strangers around the world have crafted the fabric that touches us.

This book will tell you the full story behind fashion – from the ways fabrics are sourced to how the clothes end up in your wardrobe, and what happens to them if we don't want them any more. By familiarizing yourself with this story, you are empowering yourself to make informed choices about what you wear and the clothes that you already own. We'll start by looking at the life cycle of a simple white T-shirt . . .

LIFE CYCLE OF A T-SHIRT

Everyone has at least one T-shirt in their wardrobe, but its life doesn't just begin when we wear it. In fact, it will have travelled all around the world and passed through at least 100 pairs of human hands before we've even tried it on. How often do we think about where our clothes come from, what they are made of and the impact our choice of clothes has on the world around us?

We can gather some information about the T-shirt from the care label on the inside, but it only reveals so much. For instance, the country on the label is only where the cutting, sewing and finishing happens in a garment factory. It is very unlikely that this will be the same country where the fabric is woven, dyed or even where the cotton is grown. Let's follow this life cycle of a standard T-shirt to start to understand its impact on the world . . .

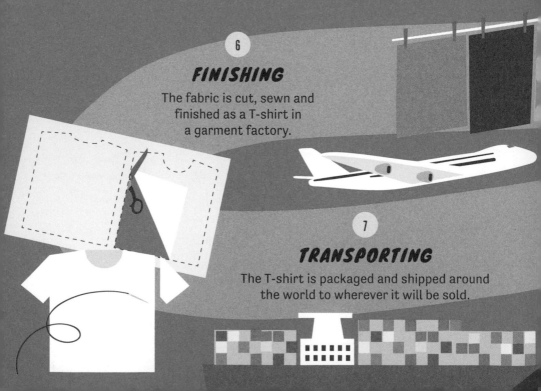

6

FINISHING

The fabric is cut, sewn and finished as a T-shirt in a garment factory.

7

TRANSPORTING

The T-shirt is packaged and shipped around the world to wherever it will be sold.

Follow the journey . . .

1

GROWING

The cotton plant is grown on a farm where its fruit or 'bolls' are harvested.

2

GINNING

The hard wooden stalk and shell are removed from the soft boll at a 'gin'.

3

SPINNING

The bolls are cleaned, pulled apart and spun into thread at a spinning mill.

4

WEAVING

The cotton thread is woven into fabric on looms in a textile mill.

5

DYEING

The cotton fabric is dyed or printed at the textile mill.

8

SELLING

The T-shirt is distributed into shops.

9

WEARING

You buy the T-shirt, wear and wash it.

This book will help you to decide what to do with clothes that you've already bought or ones you're about to buy. Mindful choices make a difference.

BUILT TO WASTE

So you buy something, and then after a couple of wears and washes the colours start to fade, threads snap, fabric goes bobbly, holes appear, the item shrinks or becomes misshapen. You looked after it, but it's beyond repair and already unwearable. What went wrong?

This is called 'planned obsolescence'. It means that something is designed to be unusable after only a short life. It is a way for companies to make people purchase things again and again and replace products more quickly.

IT CREATES AN ENDLESS DEMAND, DRIVING A DEVASTING CYCLE OF EXTRACTING MORE AND MORE PRECIOUS RAW MATERIALS FROM THE EARTH.

Fast fashion is one of the worst offenders with some fashion brands choosing to cut corners in manufacturing, poor-quality fabrics, cheaper fastenings and finishings to keep costs low. This is common practice in mass production where quantity rules over quality. Businesses can argue that it makes no sense for their customer to wear something for a long time when clothes can be as disposable as a single-use plastic bag, a coffee cup or a plastic straw . . . but we know what impact these have on the planet. Campaigners argue that planned obsolescence has to STOP.

Disposable Planet?

Look around you, and you will discover that you are surrounded by objects that have been proven to have planned obsolescence, especially electrical and electronic goods. A simple light bulb is the most famous example – even though it is possible to make one that doesn't ever go out, manufacturers make them out of cheaper materials so that they only burn for around 1,500 hours. We don't think about it when we change a light bulb because the item is relatively inexpensive, but other items carry a higher price.

TRAINERS
560 kilometres

LIGHT BULB
1,500 hours

Tights

GOLD-PLATED EARRINGS
Less than 12 months

PAIR OF TIGHTS
Sometimes just one wear

SLOW PHONES

In 2018, Apple were taken to court by French prosecutors for allegedly slowing their older iPhones down through a software update, causing people to need to buy new ones. Apple lost the case and apologized for their wrongdoing. It's also been claimed that ink-cartridge manufacturers include a smart chip in their product that stops printers using ink after a certain number of pages.

MOBILE PHONE
2 years

FAST FASHION

It's estimated that we're now manufacturing 100 billion garments annually. Some fashion brands can even produce an item of clothing, from placing the order in a factory to selling it, in as little as 36 hours. Fast fashion is the term used to describe the section of the fashion industry that focuses on cheap, disposable clothing which is produced and consumed at an alarmingly fast rate. Buy it, wear it once or twice and then throw it in the bin.

The rise of fast fashion in Western societies sees clothes continue to decrease in price despite the cost of raw materials rising. We can now buy a garment for less than the price of a coffee, yet the cost of this short turnaround of clothing is putting a huge strain on the people involved in the supply chains making our clothes, not to mention the environment.

Mass-produced clothes made in large volumes can be made far quicker and more cheaply than one-off pieces. This is called economy of scale.

NEW!

In fast fashion, clothes are produced on an assembly line where each worker will focus entirely on only one part of a T-shirt. They might spend their days sewing up the side seams or only inserting sleeves. They will never learn how to make a whole T-shirt from start to finish, and in many cases workers are overworked and underpaid.

Fashion works in cycles: what's hot and what's not. It is no longer dictated by two seasons of spring/summer and autumn/winter each year. Now we see new ranges of clothes in the shops every single week. The speed at which new trends come out encourages us to view, wear and use our clothes at a faster pace. This fuels overconsumption.

'Perceived obsolescence' is when we see that something we own is no longer stylish and believe it is out of date even if it still functions well. We may feel pressure to not be seen wearing something more than once. Conveniently, buying clothes at the click of a button, 24 hours a day, seven days a week means there is always demand and no rest for the consumer.

sale

JUST £5!

Think about trainers, and how many times brands will introduce new colours or styles to the same product every year, knowing we'll want the latest one.

ARE YOU A CONSCIOUS CONSUMER?

Some people enjoy shopping, some people don't, but at some point in our lives we all buy and consume stuff. To be a conscious consumer means being aware that the money you spend has an impact on people and the planet, for better or worse. Whether it's buying from a local independent designer or spending your money on something that has been made out of recycled materials, we have power as consumers, and we should use that power wisely.

WHEN TO SHOP?

Stop before you shop for new clothes. Ask yourself if there is another way and use our Conscious Consumer Toolkit to help you decide if you even *need* to buy a new item of clothing . . .

CONSCIOUS CONSUMER TOOLKIT

1

WEAR WHAT YOU HAVE p22

Review your wardrobe to rediscover hidden gems in the clothes you've already bought.

2

MAKE DO AND MEND p40

Set up a clothes swap with your friends, family and even your community. See what hidden gems they might have.

3

WEAR WHAT OTHERS HAVE WORN p58

Buy from a charity shop, car boot sale, flea market, auction website or vintage boutique.

4

NEW TO YOU p70

DIY, customize, cut, sew, stitch, repurpose, restyle, repair, alter and adapt. Get creative!

5

NEW NEW p86

Can't find the answer in any of the above? Buy, but choose wisely.

MINDFUL SHOPPING

This flow chart has been designed to help you be mindful when you go shopping for clothes. It's a slower and more thoughtful way to shop and will help you make the right ethical decisions for you.

START YOUR SHOPPING JOURNEY

Do you LOVE it?

NO → **Do you need it?**

Do you need it?

NO → **Don't buy it!** Why are you even asking??

YES → Sometimes we have to shop for things we need every day that are practical purchases, such as sports kit or socks. Make sure you buy the best quality you can so that they last a long time.

Does it fit you?

NO → **Don't buy it!** Unless you have the time and skills to alter it, let it go, as there's something else out there you'll love just as much.

YES → **Do you have something similar?**

Do you have something similar?

YES → **Don't buy it!** Unless the similar item is worn out and cannot be repaired, leave it.

NO → **Can you afford it?**

Can you afford it?

NO → **Is it likely you will wear this only once?**

YES → **Will you wear it more than 30 times?**

Will you wear it more than 30 times?

NO → **Is it likely you will wear this only once?**

YES → **Is it good quality?**

Is it good quality?

A MATERIAL WORLD
See page 104

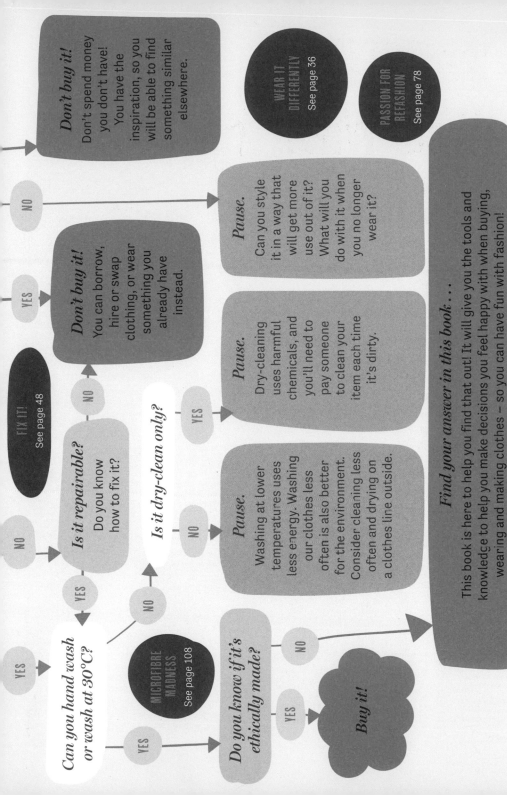

Don't buy it!
Don't spend money you don't have! You have the inspiration, so you will be able to find something similar elsewhere.

WEAR IT DIFFERENTLY
See page 36

PASSION FOR REFASHION
See page 78

Don't buy it!
You can borrow, hire or swap clothing, or wear something you already have instead.

Pause.
Can you style it in a way that will get more use out of it? What will you do with it when you no longer wear it?

Pause.
Dry-cleaning uses harmful chemicals, and you'll need to pay someone to clean your item each time it's dirty.

NO

YES

FIX IT!
See page 48

NO

Is it repairable?
Do you know how to fix it?

Is it dry-clean only?

YES

Pause.
Washing at lower temperatures uses less energy. Washing our clothes less often is also better for the environment. Consider cleaning less often and drying on a clothes line outside.

NO

NO

Can you hand wash or wash at 30°C?

YES

MICROFIBRE MADNESS
See page 108

NO

YES

Do you know if it's ethically made?

NO

YES

Buy it!

Find your answer in this book . . .
This book is here to help you find that out! It will give you the tools and knowledge to help you make decisions you feel happy with when buying, wearing and making clothes – so you can have fun with fashion!

PART ONE

Wear What You Have

Want to know what the most sustainable item of clothing is? It's . . . the one you already own! Buying nothing is kind to our current and future planet (and it's also kind to your bank balance).

Woven into the fabric of the clothes that already exist in our homes are huge amounts of energy, water, land-use and chemicals. According to the Sustainable Clothing Action Plan (SCAP), extending the use of our clothes by just nine months would reduce their carbon, water and waste footprints by 20 to 30 per cent. So by wearing what we already have and not buying new, we can collectively tackle the problem of throwaway fashion. We can avoid overconsumption of our planet's precious, finite resources – and reduce unnecessary waste.

WOULD YOU BE SURPRISED TO LEARN THAT THE AVERAGE PERSON HAS AROUND 150 GARMENTS HANGING IN THEIR WARDROBE?

What about the fact that we've not worn a third of those clothes in the last year? And what about the clothes that we buy and never wear? Many of us are guilty of buying something we don't really need as a treat to cheer ourselves up, or as a reward for doing something. We've all fallen for an item in the sale because it was too good a bargain to miss, or bought something that doesn't fit because we hope one day it will. All of these garments hang with their shop tags still attached, unworn and unloved at the back of the wardrobe, until we admit we'll never wear them and pass them on to someone else.

In this section we'll be delving into the deep, dark depths of your wardrobe to get the most out of what you already have . . . .

A good wardrobe clear-out is a great way to start making a more sustainable collection of clothes. You'll be keeping the clothes you love and giving the clothes you don't love the chance of a new life.

Top tips to clearing out your clothes:

Give yourself enough time! And space. You need to make a mess to create order.

Invite a friend round for a second opinion. They'll help you part with those bad shopping choices and press you for honest answers on the plans you have for certain items.

Marie Kondo, the tidying guru, recommends getting all your clothes together in one place so you can see what you're dealing with. This includes clothes hiding under your bed and any lurking in the washing basket.

Seeing your clothes all together will highlight your shopping patterns. Maybe you didn't realize you had 20 pairs of jeans, ten stripy tops or everything in blue. You might even rediscover forgotten clothes!

Try on everything in the pile! See if it fits you.

Create a 'yes' and 'no' pile. Hang or fold the 'yes's neatly, and use our Think-Before-You-Bin guide (page 26) to deal with the 'no' pile.

PUT TOGETHER

Clearing out your wardrobe will help you spot new clothes combinations to wear. Try storing clothes by colour or type to make it easy to create new put-together looks. Or even group complete tried-and-tested outfits together for a grab-and-go style.

REMEMBER:

Aim to discard clothes you haven't worn in over a year and clothes that don't make you feel happy. Be honest about how much you wear each item. We often get emotionally attached to clothes, which can make it hard to part with them, but be strong! Remember you might not get the same thrill from practical clothes, such as sports kit or wardrobe staples, but if you use them they should stay. It's worth keeping special-occasion outfits to save you buying them again.

THINK BEFORE YOU BIN

Once you've edited your collection of clothes you're left with the ones you know you'll wear. So what do you do with the rest? Should you donate them, sell them or take them to the local recycling centre? This guide will help you decide . . .

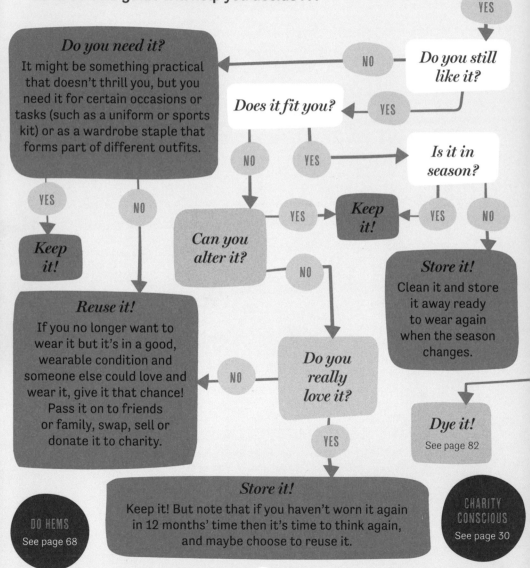

YES

Do you still like it?

NO

Do you need it?
It might be something practical that doesn't thrill you, but you need it for certain occasions or tasks (such as a uniform or sports kit) or as a wardrobe staple that forms part of different outfits.

Does it fit you?

YES

YES **NO**

Is it in season?

YES

NO

Keep it!

YES **NO**

Can you alter it?

YES

NO

Keep it!

Store it!
Clean it and store it away ready to wear again when the season changes.

Reuse it!
If you no longer want to wear it but it's in a good, wearable condition and someone else could love and wear it, give it that chance! Pass it on to friends or family, swap, sell or donate it to charity.

NO

Do you really love it?

YES

Dye it!
See page 82

Store it!
Keep it! But note that if you haven't worn it again in 12 months' time then it's time to think again, and maybe choose to reuse it.

DO HEMS
See page 68

CHARITY CONSCIOUS
See page 30

START HERE

Is it in good condition?
Are all buttons present and fastenings working? The condition might be affected by holes, stains, rips, dropped hems, worn-through fabric, fraying or pilling (tiny bobbles on the surface of the fabric). Can the garment be worn?

NO →

Can you fix it?
Assess how bad the damage is and be a mending activist. What's the problem?

STAINED

Could you creatively embellish it to hide the stain?

NO **YES**

Fix it!
See page 80

Is it made out of at least 50% natural fibres?

YES **NO**

BOBBLED

Fix it!
Pilling can appear on the fabric's surface from washing and wear. Some fabrics pill more than others. Try using an electronic fabric shaver or use some sticky tape to remove the bobbles.

Could someone wear it?
If it's lost shape for you, could it still fit someone else?

NO **YES**

Swap it!
See page 60

STRETCHED

MISSING BUTTONS, TORN, BROKEN ZIP OR HOLES

Can you sew?
Simple repairs, such as missing buttons, holes that need patching or seams that have split, can easily be solved with some basic sewing.

NO **YES**

Fix it!
See page 48

DO BUTTONS
See page 64

FASHION FIX
See page 48

Can someone else fix it?
You could try taking it to a repair café.

YES **NO**

Recycle it!
Take it to your local clothes recycling centre, or check online to see where your nearest textile bank is. Your item can be turned into things such as car-seat stuffing, engineering rags or insulation. Or you can recycle it yourself by using the fabric for craft projects, stuffing for cushions or even as cleaning rags at home.

SELL YOUR CLOTHES

Give your unwanted, unloved, unworn clothes the chance of a new life, and make money too! Follow these simple steps and you're just a few clicks away from an international marketplace.

1

KNOW WHICH SITE OR APP IS RIGHT FOR YOU

There are lots of websites and apps out there, and we've provided a list of the best ones at the back of this book (see page 148). Certain clothes and brands will sell better on different sites, so do your research and see which one best suits you and your product. (You'll also need permission from a parent or guardian to set up an account.) Check commission fees too – this is the fee the site takes for enabling the sale. An average is ten per cent – meaning if you sell something for £20 the site takes ten per cent (£2) and you'll get £18.

2

WASH AND IRON CLOTHES BEFORE YOU SELL

Present your clothes in the best possible condition. That means no stains, wrinkles or horrible surprises! Only sell clothes that you think someone would pay money for and actually want to wear.

3

TAKE THE BEST PHOTOS POSSIBLE

Your customer can't feel the fabric or try the item on before they buy so they need to understand what it looks like through your excellent photography skills. Try using a model so your customer can see how it looks. Or lie the item on a plain flat surface and take a photo from above. Using well-positioned lamps can help get rid of any shadows. Take a few photos from different angles and make sure there is no clutter in the background. If your garment has any flaws then make sure you take close-ups to avoid disappointments or even disputes.

4
IT'S ALL IN THE DETAIL

Be clear and be honest. Include brand, size, colour and condition in your product title and a description so it's easy to search and find. You need to keep a good reputation as a seller, so be honest about any problems with the item, such as it being small for the labelled size, but be sure to mention any nice features too.

5
SHIPPING COSTS

Always get proof of postage, even if you don't pay for signed-for or tracked posting. Lots of sites will let you list the postage cost separatcly, but if you don't have this option make sure you add this to your total price. Weigh the item and work out how much it will cost to post.

6
PRICE TO SELL

Do your homework and check what other similar items have sold for. Don't go too high or too low but check competition and think about what you believe is a fair price. On some sites you can sell at a fixed price, set up an auction or invite the buyer to make an offer. If your item isn't selling, you can consider reducing the price, changing the description or rephotographing it.

Some websites and apps will collect the items, photograph them and sell them for you without the hassle, but check their fees.

CHARITY CONSCIOUS

Charity shops provide a vital service, keeping clothes and accessories that can be used again out of the trash, and in doing so, raising money for good causes. They are a perfect example of the circular economy where reusing beats recycling (see page 114).

Whilst charity shops rely on donations of good-quality items, they are increasingly receiving stock from the fashion industry. These donations might be 'deadstock' – clothes from previous seasons that haven't sold – or 'seconds' that may have a flaw. Some popular fashion labels have hit the headlines for incinerating or slashing these clothes, so it's far better for their ethical record if this stock goes to charity.

Although it might seem like an act of generosity, in recent years, charity shops have become fashion dumping grounds. They have become inundated with cheap fast fashion that no one wants to wear second-hand, and deadstock clothes no one wanted to wear first-hand. This means that charity shops are forced to find a way to get rid of them responsibly.

Charities often sell unsaleable stock on to rag merchants or recycling companies. What they do with them can change from business to business, but the stock may be sent overseas or recycled into something else. It is worth asking a charity where your donations are going – the end of the supply chain is just as important as the beginning.

Increasingly, fashion brands are asking their customers to donate unwanted clothes through 'bring back' schemes in-store. It's an easy way for them to meet sustainability goals and appeal to customers who would like their favourite brands to care more for the environment. With promises of reducing waste, and some even claiming to recycle donations into new products, it's a positive move in the right direction. However, a lot of brands offer incentives as a reward for returning clothes in the form of vouchers to buy something new. This is arguably environmentally counter-productive and negates the positive impact of using our clothes as much as we can.

WHAT A WASTE

In the UK alone, over a million tonnes of clothes are thrown away each year, with 300,000 tonnes (equivalent to £140 million worth of clothes) heading to landfill. In comparison, the United States discards a staggering 15 million tonnes, with only 15 per cent being reused and recycled whilst the rest is buried or burnt . . .

Depending on where you live, any clothes you throw away into household waste will end up in landfill or be incinerated (burnt at very high temperatures). Both are terrible for the planet. In landfill, as clothes break down, those made of natural fibres give off methane, a greenhouse gas that is contributing to climate change. When incinerated, the valuable materials in clothes are lost forever.

Donating clothes to charity is great but some charities are overwhelmed with items that are not good enough to sell in their shops. They sell them by the tonne to clothes recyclers or wholesalers, who then ship them off to places such as Eastern Europe and parts of Africa where they are sold in second-hand markets. Are we just passing our waste and overconsumption problem to other parts of the world to deal with, so that we can continue shopping? What will happen to that waste if those countries stop allowing this to happen?

Even clothes that are ripped and torn beyond repair should not go in the bin. Check to see if there is a clothes recycling point near you. Clothes left there can be 'downcycled' to turn them into rags and insulation for the construction industry, which is so much better than burning or burying them in landfill. Really this is just a way of delaying the inevitable end of the life of the garment, but it does mean giving them another purpose before that happens.

It's estimated that **95%** of the textiles binned in the UK could have been reused or recycled.

Times 30?

We only have one planet with finite resources. According to WWF we currently use 1.7 times our planet's resources every year, meaning we are not conserving resources for the future. The average garment is worn fewer than ten times before being discarded, so challenge yourself to the 30-wears challenge. Wear each item at least 30 times to get more out of your clothes and reduce their impact on the planet.

FOSSIL FASHION

Take a look at the label in something you're wearing now. What is it made out of? Cotton? Lycra? Viscose? Wool? You might be surprised to learn that once it's discarded and buried in landfill, some fibres and materials break down faster than others. Let's dig a bit deeper and see.

FASHION ARCHAEOLOGY

Check out this timeline to see how long it takes for your clothes to decompose. These timings are estimates: the pH of the soil, the temperature, and the levels of moisture, oxygen and bacteria all affect the speed of the decomposition. Landfill sites often lack the conditions for materials to break down fully. Instead, our waste is packed tightly, preserving it for future generations to deal with whilst it slowly leaches dangerous chemicals into the soil and harmful gases into the atmosphere.

A FEW WEEKS
Linen vest,
silk shirt

AROUND SIX MONTHS
Cotton
T-shirt

1–5 YEARS
Wool socks,
bamboo sweatshirt

25–40 YEARS
Leather shoes

Long Live Your Wardrobe

Get out a sample of some of your favourite clothes. Check their labels, and then arrange them in order of how quickly you think they will decompose based on the timeline. Are you surprised that some of your clothes take so long to biodegrade, if at all? What impact could this have on the planet?

Wait! Now look closer at any fastenings, labels, thread, prints and embellishment on the clothing. Do you think the plastic sequins and buttons or the metal zip fastening will speed up or slow down decomposition? Do you think the designer considered that their creations might outlive them or might one day end up buried in the ground somewhere?

AROUND 30-40 YEARS
Nylon tights

200* YEARS
Lycra shorts

200+ YEARS
Polyester dress

350,000 tonnes of clothing is discarded in the UK every year – the same weight as all the clothes owned by people living in London.

Clothes that have multiple functions can help increase the number of times we wear them and how long we keep them. Sustainable-fashion stylist Alice Wilby shares her top-ten styling tips to get the most out of what you have in your wardrobe.

1 MIX CASUAL AND DRESSY ITEMS

Pair a denim shirt with a fancy skirt or tuxedo trousers for a night out. Or pop some trainers on with that dress you've only worn once to a wedding and wear them both differently.

2 GET CREATIVE . . .

. . . and turn an oversized shirt into a skirt. Step into it with the top buttons undone and tie the sleeves at the waist like a belt. This also works well for jumpers with a zip neck. Go borrow one off your dad!

3 STYLE A SKIRT OVER TROUSERS

This style is often repeated on the catwalk at great expense but looks much cooler if you DIY it. The overall shape and mix of fabrics is key to pulling this off. A-line miniskirts with flared trousers work beautifully together.

4 WEAR A SHIRT AS A JACKET

That heavy flannel or denim shirt will work really well as a summer jacket. It will look equally good when worn oversized with rolled-up sleeves.

5   LAYER THINGS UP

Layer things up. Throw a T-shirt under that strappy dress, a cropped jumper over a long shirt and a longline duster coat over the top, or try a polo neck under a shirt. Playing with layers elevates your outfits and also helps create multiple looks.

6   MIX CLASHING PRINTS

Ignore the rule of only wearing one print at a time. Have some fun mixing up pieces of your wardrobe that you'd normally wear with a plain top or bottom.

7   PLAY WITH COLOUR AND TEXTURE

Like layering and mixing prints, playing with the different colours and textures you have in your wardrobe will enable you to create outfits you'd not thought about before.

8   RAID SOMEONE ELSE'S WARDROBE

So many brands have a unisex vibe and some have even started making genderless collections. But you don't have to shell out for this, just have a rifle through a friend's wardrobe (ask permission!) and style yourself up with no gender rules.

9   ACCESSORIES CHANGE EVERYTHING

Try a silk scarf worn as a belt. Cover the lapels of your jacket with brooches and badges. Or swap out the belt that comes with a coat or a dress for one that is a contrasting colour or texture.

10   TAKE PICTURES . . .

. . . of each winning outfit you've styled yourself and create your own 'image bank'. It will come in handy when you're in a rush or have completely forgotten what you've got in your wardrobe.

LET YOUR CLOTHES LIVE

More and more people are challenging themselves to 'Buy Nothing New' for a month or even a year. This money-saving activity has the added bonus of refocusing our minds on the clothes we already own and how we care for them. If we're serious about slowing down our consumption and reducing our environmental footprint, then we need to learn how to care for our clothes properly. They might not be glamorous, but these small everyday acts of maintenance let our treasured clothes live and thrive.

ACT WITH CARE AND INVEST IN WHAT YOU HAVE WITH THESE TIPS:

SMART STORAGE

- Clean, fold and store out-of-season clothes to make space for what is in use.

- Fold clothes along the seams to avoid creasing and wear and tear.

- Avoid plastic vacuum-pack bags (even if they do save space).

- Use acid-free tissue or alternatively store clothes in old cotton pillowcases to let them breathe.

- Store clothes away from damp, direct sunlight or heat.

- Avoid wire hangers that can damage clothes, and never hang knitwear.

- Learn some basic mending skills in the next part of this book!

FREEZER FRESH

- Freshen up jeans in the freezer for a few days instead of washing them.

- A problem with moths can be treated by washing, bagging and freezing knitwear for two weeks to kill the larvae that will feast on your clothes and create holes. (Always do this before storing knitwear away).

Museum conservators store clothes in temperatures between 18 and 23°C.

WASHING WAYS

- Wash clothes less frequently so that they maintain their quality (see also page 108).

- Wash similar colours together, and turn jeans inside out to keep them from fading.

- Handwash vintage clothes, woollens and delicates with a light touch.

- Make sure zips are zipped and pockets are empty before washing.

- Moisturize and treat leather regularly to prevent it cracking.

- Use an electric shaver to remove pilling for a quick fabric refresh.

- Delicates and knitwear may benefit from drying flat on a towel and reshaping.

- Try hanging creased garments in a steamy bathroom instead of ironing them to save time.

- Avoid drying clothes in a machine – it causes pilling and reduces fabric strength.

PART TWO

MAKE DO AND MEND

Before our modern fast-fashion culture, especially during hard times, people have scrimped, saved and been savvy and resourceful to get the most out of the clothes they already have. Mending clothes to give them a new lease of life has happened for centuries, but war has often made it a necessity.

During World War II , the US and British governments began rationing fabric to make sure there were enough raw materials to support the war effort. The British introduced a scheme called 'Make Do and Mend' and issued leaflets encouraging people to mend and revive their old clothes.

In January 1943, even *Vogue* magazine advised readers to renovate existing clothes instead of buying new ones, which was no longer an option for most people. Today we can rediscover the principles of 'Make Do and Mend' as we wage a war on waste.

Rediscovering a lost art

Embroidery, knitting, sewing and mending were once part of any young girl's education. While it's great that girls are no longer stuck just learning domestic subjects, these are brilliant skills that are useful for everyone. Learning to sew is also a good way to become a mending activist (see page 48).

DUTY OF CARE

In the countries affected by the war, mending became a patriotic duty as well as a necessity. Old garments were cut down and remade as wartime fashion items. Due to the silk shortage, women shared formal wear and wedding dresses. With so many men away for long periods of time, women were encouraged to remake their husband's suits into garments for all the family.

Make-up and hairstyling became increasingly important as women found creative ways around war shortages, such as using boot polish for mascara. They even dyed their legs with tea and used gravy browning to draw stocking seams down the back!

WHITE WEDDING

Surplus parachute silks were sometimes repurposed into wedding dresses, although the 'silk' was actually nylon or rayon. Brides could avoid wearing white altogether, or dye their white dresses and alter them after their weddings so they could be worn again.

WARTIME FASHION

In wartime, or in other times of great hardship, is there any place for the fun and frivolity of fashion? During World War II, clothes and fabric were in short supply, and there were all sorts of restrictions on what people could wear.

Rationing was introduced to make sure necessities such as food, fuel and clothes were shared out fairly. In Britain, the government introduced a scheme called 'Utility clothing'. The plan was to minimise waste while making sure clothes were of reasonable quality. Top fashion designers were asked to create a range of clothing under strict rules.

Pleats were banned, no more than two pockets and five buttons were allowed and clothes had to have reinforced seams to ensure they would last. Men's shirts had a maximum length, suits could only be single breasted and there was a ban on trouser turn-ups too. Advertising campaigns were used to shame wasteful behaviour and even suggest that extravagant dress was unpatriotic.

UTILITY STYLE

Many women took to wearing Utility Jumpsuits during the war because they were useful and easy to pull on. The jumpsuit, a new invention, was warm, comfortable and had all-important pockets.

TROUSER TRIBE

Trousers were worn by women who worked in factories during the war, and they soon gained in popularity. The US actress Katherine Hepburn appeared in several movies wearing elegant, wide-legged trousers and the trend took off.

The popularity of trousers for women didn't end when the war did.

THE NEW LOOK

The years of rationing changed people's behaviour and attitudes to fashion. After the war, designer Christian Dior caused quite a stir in Paris with his 'New Look', with nipped-in waists, shoulder pads and very full skirts. Many people considered the huge amounts of fabric he used to be in bad taste after their years of austerity.

BORO TEXTILE JACKET

タール

JAPANESE COOL

Some of the most influential, iconic and innovative fashion designers in the world have come out of Japan, such as Issey Miyake, Yohji Yamamoto, Junya Watanabe and Rei Kawakubo.

Japanese fashion design embraces modernity and technology whilst respecting its rich and distinctive historical traditions. One of those traditions, the patching and repairing of garments, or *Boro*, was born out of necessity.

BORO TEXTILES

Boro, meaning 'tattered rags', dates back to Japan's Edo period (1603–1868), when fabric was costly and scarce. Certain fabrics, such as silk or any brightly coloured and patterned textiles, were only available to the wealthy. Even small scraps of fabric were costly and people had little alternative but to repair the clothes they already had themselves.

Boro refers to garments and quilts that have been patched and repaired over many years and passed down through generations as heirlooms. As holes appeared in an item or the fabric wore thin, scraps of fabric – indigo-dyed cotton, linen or hemp – were patchworked on top of each other and stitched.

CONTINUOUS PATCHING SERVED TO TELL AN ITEM'S STORY AND CREATE A PRECIOUS HEIRLOOM IN JAPANESE FAMILIES.

At the turn of the 19th century, working-class Japanese people discarded their Boro garments as they now had higher living standards and were embarrassed about the poverty they had been living in. Boro was a reflection of this and little was done by the government to preserve the garments or the Boro tradition.

Now these garments fetch huge sums at auction and are displayed in art galleries. Antique or vintage Boro have become valuable collectors' items, and Boro has inspired a new trend in modern mending.

DO SASHIKO

BECOME A MENDING ACTIVIST!

Sashiko means 'little stabs' in Japanese. It refers to the stitching on indigo-dyed cloth and can be seen on items of Boro. Sashiko can be used to reinforce and repair fabric that has worn thin or applied to pressure points on a garment, such as elbows and knees, to strengthen these areas and prevent them wearing out too quickly. It is also used decoratively: small running stitches made using white embroidery thread are used to create a pattern of small broken lines or dashes.

Inspired to have a go and add some sashiko to your clothes so that they last longer? Find some classic patterns at the back of this book to get you started . . .

WHAT YOU WILL NEED:

- Fabric or garment to embroider on to
- Long sashiko needle (*or long darning needle*)
- White sashiko or embroidery thread (*although you could try out different contrasting colours if you like*)
- Ruler (if drawing pattern freehand)
- Tailor's chalk

- Pins
- Pen or pencil for tracing
- Printout of your pattern template (*you can use the examples at the back of this book, find more online or create your own*)
- Fabric scissors
- Embroidery hoop (*optional*)

METHOD:

1 Select a pattern. You can choose your own or use one of the three sashiko patterns shown at the back of this book: the highlighted squares show a single tile – repeat the pattern as much as you need to.

2 Lay paper pattern print on top of the garment and make tiny pin pricks along the pattern lines. Rub tailor's chalk over the pattern to transfer the chalk markings through the holes in the pattern on to the garment.

3 Go over the pattern on the fabric with tailor's chalk so you can see the pattern clearly. Remember the chalk rubs off so don't worry if you make a mistake! Alternatively, draw freehand on to the fabric using a ruler where necessary and skip step 2.

4 Place the garment in an embroidery hoop if you have one. Thread the needle and tie a knot in the end.

5 Stitch a basic small running stitch up and down on to the fabric, following the lines of your pattern. The stitches should look like lots of small dashes or a broken line, evenly spaced.

6 When you are finished, push the needle to the back and turn garment over to the wrong side. Pick up a small bit of fabric (not all the way through) or pick up a previous stitch to create a new loop. Put the needle through this loop and pull to form a knot. Repeat twice.

RUNNING STITCH

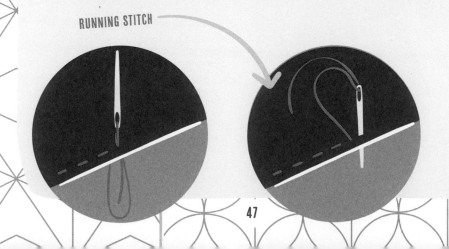

FASHION FIX

When something is broken, don't just throw it in the bin. Try fixing it first! There are plenty of ideas to get you started in this book, but if you're someone that learns better from someone else, or you can't find the advice you need here or online, then a repair café might literally be up your street.

A repair café is a free community event where you can learn how to fix your stuff with the help of volunteers who have the skills to share. The first one was started in Amsterdam in 2009 by journalist Martine Postma and there are now thousands of repair events happening globally, from repair cafés to restart parties and fix-it clinics.

ANYTHING GOES

You can take electrical items and bikes as well as clothes, and sometimes even furniture, to a repair café. There are always more broken things than there are volunteers who know how to help you fix them, so arrive early and be patient. You might have to wait, but it will be worth it!

Could YOU be a mending activist?

A mending activist is someone who uses their skills to actively reduce consumption and waste. A mending activist doesn't just fix their own stuff but wants to help others too. A mending activist will not be defeated — so if they can't fix it themselves they will seek advice from others who can. A mending activist's work is never done, as there will always be more stuff to fix.

You don't need to have a fashion degree to know how to repair clothes. As long as you have some of the following attributes then you've got all the foundations to be a mending activist.

YOU NEED TO:

- be confident taking things apart
- enjoy problem-solving
- have good hand-eye coordination (haptic skills) . . .
- . . . and a sprinkling of creativity.

HOW CAN YOU FIND OUT IF THERE'S A REPAIR CAFÉ NEAR YOU?

Local online forums and social media are good places to start. Lots of repair cafés happen in libraries and community centres, so look out for posters or leaflets there.

See page 149 for how to find your own local repair café.

MAKE-DO-AND-MEND TOOLKIT

Here's a set of items that every mending activist might need in their repair kit . . .

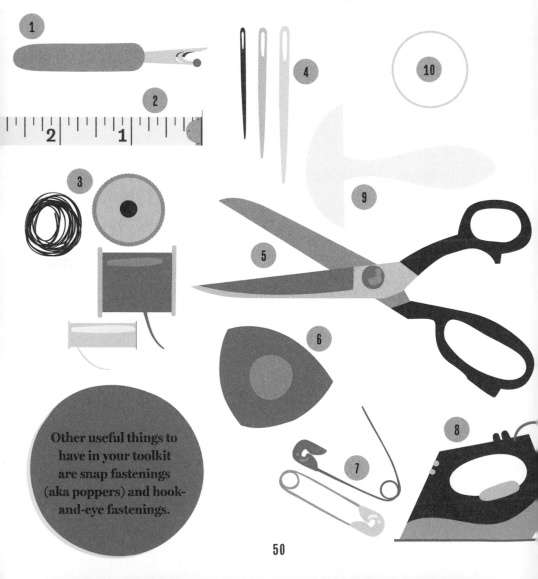

Other useful things to have in your toolkit are snap fastenings (aka poppers) and hook-and-eye fastenings.

HERE'S A LIST OF THE STAPLE SEWING ACCESSORIES AND GADGETS THAT MAKE UP A REALLY USEFUL TOOLKIT.

1. Seam ripper aka 'unpicker'
To remove unwanted stitches.

2. Measuring tape
A flexible tape to measure fabric and take body measurements.

3. Assorted coloured thread and yarn
Thread and yarn will be used for stitching, embroidery and darning.

4. Selection of sewing needles
Needles are used for hand sewing and come in varying sizes.

5. Fabric scissors
To cut fabric. (Make sure no one takes your fabric scissors to cut paper with, as it blunts them!)

6. Tailor's chalk or fabric marker
To make temporary markings on fabric that can be rubbed off or washed off.

7. Safety pins
For temporary fastening.

8. Iron
To press seams, remove creases and iron on patches before sewing.

9. Darning mushroom
To provide a hard, curved surface for darning knitwear.

10. Double-sided iron-on adhesive
Useful for temporarily fusing fabric together with the iron before stitching in place.

11. Thimble
To protect your finger as you push a needle through fabric.

12. Snips
Small scissors to cut threads and yarn.

13. Pins
To hold fabric in place while sewing.

Think about starting a collection of scrap fabrics, buttons and zips. If you catch someone you know getting rid of clothes that are ripped and tattered beyond repair, save some of the fabric and fastenings to add to your stock cupboard for future projects.

DO PATCHING

Ideally, you would reinforce worn fabric before a hole appears in it with some sashiko stitching (see page 46) but if a hole does appear, why not get creative with a patch and put your mending activism into practice? A patch can be invisible or visible depending on where it is, the fabric you use and the look that you want.

1 Cut the fabric patch so it's easily large enough to cover the hole and any thin areas around the hole.

2 Fold over the edges of the patch by 0.5–1cm, and press with an iron. (Please be careful when using an iron.)

Build a library of assorted fabric swatches for future projects. Rifle through old clothes, duvet covers, curtains and even tablecloths to rescue any useful or interesting materials before recycling them. Don't forget to unpick zips, remove other fastenings and salvage beautiful trims as they may come in handy too!

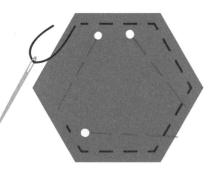

3 Pin the patch on to your garment and tack with a large running stitch to hold in place. Remove pins.

Sew a blanket stitch or whip stitch along the edge of the patch and finish with a knot.

Take care to thread the needle back through each loop with every stitch.

BLANKET STITCH

Sew the stitches on a 45° angle.

WHIP STITCH

Try and choose patch fabric that is a similar weight to your garment. You can take it from inside a pocket to get an exact match.

5 Remove the running stitches – and wear proudly!

INSPIRING PATCHES

Patchwork is a great way to use up small scraps of fabric. Piece together pieces of fabric to create a larger piece of fabric to make a garment. Alternatively, add layers of coloured patches on to an existing garment to update it, hide problem areas or simply to make something unique to you.

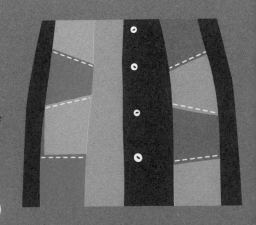

DO DARNING

If you have unwanted holes in your knitwear or indeed any woven material, then darning can be the answer to get your clothes looking new again. It can be used instead of patching to mend worn garments and is a darn good life skill to learn.

Reinforce thin areas of fabric with Swiss darning. A bit like embroidery, it imitates the knitted stitches to strengthen them.

DARNING MUSHROOM

WHAT YOU WILL NEED:

- Darning mushroom (*or you can use a small ceramic bowl, tennis ball or anything small with a hard, curved edge*)
- Long darning needle
- Wool, yarn or embroidery thread
- Scissors or snips (*special little scissors handy for snipping close-up details*)

1 When choosing thread, choose one that is a similar thickness to the knitted garment you are mending.

2 Thread the needle with the wool but do not knot the end.

3 Turn the garment inside out, and place the darning mushroom (or curved object) underneath the hole that needs darning. Try not to stretch the garment too tightly.

4 Start at the bottom-left edge of the hole. You will need to reinforce the area around the hole, so start approximately two or three rows of stitches to the left and below the hole or worn area.

START

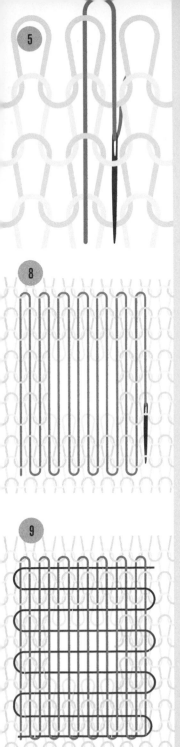

5 Follow the natural rows in the knitwear working from bottom to top. Using the tip of the needle, pick up the upward-facing loops and weave the threaded needle over and under.

6 When you reach the top edge of the hole pull the needle through. Make sure to leave a 2cm tail of thread at the end.

7 Next pick up the downward-pointing loops in the next row working in the opposite direction (from bottom to top in this instance). When you reach the end, pull through. Leave little loops at the end of each row to allow for shrinkage.

8 Repeat this process up and down vertically going from left to right across the hole until it's completely covered.

9 Next, weave the thread in and out horizontally picking up the vertical threads you've made. Ensure you alternate going over and under to create a neatly woven crosshatched patch with no gaps.

10 When you come to the end leave another tail (no need to knot).

11 Weave in the loose ends. Put a needle on the yarn (end) and pick up a few stitches diagonally, and trim. Repeat for all ends.

12 Your darning should look like this!

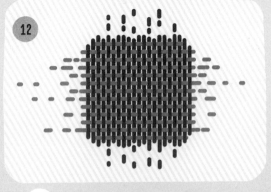

VISIBLE MENDING

There are two types of mending: visible and invisible, but a repair is always functional. The approach to a repair depends on what the garment is, what it is made out of, where the problem area is, how it's been used and will be used in its next stage of life. It will also impact the final look of it.

Whilst the main purpose of repairing something is driven by economic and increasingly environmental factors, in recent years the visible-mending movement has boomed. These are menders that welcome the opportunity to not just optimize their wardrobe and fix their loved clothes when they are broken, but to actually use the repair to highlight that they've worn the garment enough to warrant sitting down and spending time to mend it. Prominent visible menders Celia Pym, Tom of Holland, Bridget Harvey and Amy Twigger Holroyd have embraced this art form that arguably makes the repaired garment even more beautiful than it was before.

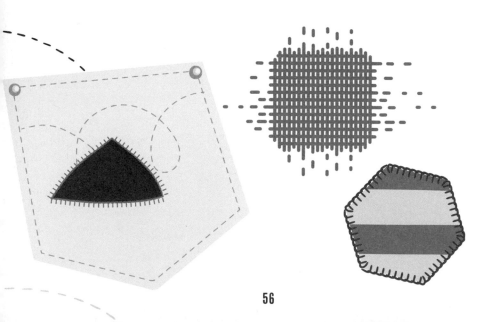

Wabi sabi is a Japanese philosophy meaning to see the beauty of things imperfect, impermanent, incomplete and unconventional. It's the opposite of the sterile clean lines of modern-day living with abundant Instagram filters and careful curation. This philosophy can be applied to our clothes. When clothes are loved and lived-in they evolve over time to become frayed, stained, worn and torn, taking on an appearance that is unique to the individual. A hole here and an unravel there might trigger emotions and memories of experiences lived in them, so a repair is just an inevitable stage in the life of our clothes.

So next time you have a hole in a garment, why not see it as an opportunity to make a feature of it? Try darning in a bold contrasting colour so it stands out and shows everyone you've taken the time to care for and repair your clothes. You could employ some clever embroidery or beadwork to highlight the repair, or even blanket stitch around the edge in a different colour thread to keep the hole and emphasize it! It'll certainly be a talking point and might inspire others to repair their clothes too.

Mindful Mending

Mending clothes enables us to take the time out of our day to slow down, relax, reflect and reconnect. The rhythmic repetitive act of crafting is calming and can promote positive mental health and a sense of wellbeing away from the pressures of everyday life.

PART THREE

Wear What Others Have Worn

You've mined your wardrobe but still really really need (or want) another piece of clothing. Don't go shopping just yet! One of the easiest ways of getting new clothes and styles is by wearing what others have. By borrowing, sharing and swapping with others, we can tap into new looks without spending any money or damaging the environment.

Swapping can be a brilliant way of meeting like-minded people with a shared clothing style. It can bring

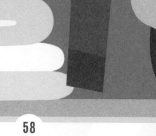

communities together as well as giving clothes a new lease of life. For some of you, borrowing and swapping clothes might already be second nature if you're lucky enough to have siblings or other family members with great taste in clothes. That friend who has a style you admire might not mind sharing the contents of their wardrobe in exchange for access to yours, if you ask nicely. Swapping also lets you experiment with styles, silhouettes and sizes, learning how to style, and accessorize and test a new look without the commitment of spending money.

Understanding sizing and simple alterations can increase your chances of tapping into some gems. To wear what others have may require some gentle persuasion and an open mind, but it can open the door to a new wardrobe of possibilities and a whole new look for you.

NO SWEAT SWAP

Something that leads us to shy away from wearing second-hand clothing is not knowing where the clothes come from, even though we probably don't know where our new ones come from either! There is an intimacy to wearing clothes as they sit against our skin, but remember, clothes can be washed. If you're still not convinced about buying second-hand, then swapping clothes with your friends, or borrowing them, is a great place to start.

Our peers can be our number-one influencers when it comes to what we wear. Borrowing an outfit from a friend allows you to experiment with a new style without the financial commitment. Of course, if you borrow something, you should look after it as if it were your own. And make sure you return it! No piece of clothing is worth falling out over.

Clothes swaps provide a great way to pass on the clothes you're no longer wearing and exchange them for something you will wear. Why not invite your friends round for a fun evening of sharing wardrobe items they no longer want? Either you'll see your unwanted clothes in a new light, or you'll find a treasure trove in your friends' collections. Run clothes swaps regularly and you may never need to buy new clothes again!

SWAPPING RULES:

Whether you swap with friends at home or go along to a larger community clothes swap (see page 62), here are some ground rules:

- Only take clean clothes in good condition.

- Always try items on first.

- Don't take something home that you're not 100 per cent sure about because you'll just be adding to your unwanted-clothes pile.

- Don't stress if an item you like doesn't fit – put it back and find another.

- Be happy that your old clothes have gone to a good home.

COMMUNITY CLOTHES SWAP

If you really want to reduce the impact of new-clothes buying in your community, you can maximize your friend clothes swap by turning it into a community-wide one.

HERE'S HOW TO DO IT:

1 FIND A VENUE

A school hall, library, café, gallery, religious centre or community hall is a good choice for a clothes swap. Some venues may be happy for you to use their space for free, but you may need to rent the space. If you do have to pay, you may wish to sell tickets or charge a small amount on the door to recover the cost.

2 PROMOTE THE EVENT

Your posters and flyers should include date, time, venue, ticket price (if not free), a short explanation of what a clothes swap is and what people can bring. Display these in places with high footfall and visibility, such as supermarkets and cafés (ask permission first). Utilize social media. Share news of your swap event with your networks, tap in to the venue's network and local community. Update regularly to maintain interest and also contact local press to advertise.

3 'TEAM CLOTHES SWAP'

You will need help on the day setting up, sorting clothes and packing away. Ask friends and family, and assign tasks to each team member. You will need one or two on 'reception' to check the clothes in, another to oversee the changing area and someone to manage the swap area. Pick a team colour to wear on the day so people know who to ask for help.

4 MAKE YOUR SWAP A SUCCESS

- How are you going to display the clothes? Rails and hangers are ideal. Ask around, and put a request online. See if a local clothes shop or even a theatre group have any you can borrow for the day. No rails? Check if the venue has tables to display the clothes on. Or fashion a clothesline from string and pegs, and put smaller items in labelled boxes.

- Speak to the venue about supplying refreshments. A local business may sponsor your event exchanging snacks for promotion. You could even ask people to bring nibbles to share.

- Make a great soundtrack to swap to.

- Have a token 'currency' to give to people in exchange for their clothes. The amount of tokens correlate to the number of items they bring, so if someone brings two items to the swap they receive two tokens and can choose no more than two garments in the swap.

- Make a changing area with a mirror, and hang sheets or a curtain for privacy.

- At the very end of the swap you may wish to give people the opportunity to purchase additional items.

- Choose a local charity shop to donate leftover clothes to, or alternatively store leftover clothes as stock for your next clothes swap.

5 ON THE DAY

- If you're expecting a lot of people, stagger drop-off and swap start times to give you and your team time to check, sort and display clothes.

- Check the clothes for quality. Look out for holes in crotches, scuffed hems, broken straps and stains around the neck, armpits and cuffs. If clothes aren't good enough for swapping, refuse the item, but offer advice on what they can do with them instead (see page 48).

- As people leave, check the number of clothes against the number of tokens to ensure a fair exchange.

Happy swapping!

SIZING UP

If you've ever felt that clothes look so much better on others than they do on you, then you're not alone. Fashion can evoke lots of emotions and sometimes they don't always leave us feeling fantastic about ourselves. In fact, a lack of body confidence can have an impact on all areas of our lives, affecting our performance at school or work and making us experience feelings of shame and guilt. We know it's not healthy to compare ourselves with the 'perfect' images we see every day, but often this is easier said than done.

Swapping clothes with other people might lead to some tricky conversations with your friends about sizes, but sizing across fashion brands isn't the same. Each brand has a target customer with a particular lifestyle and an 'ideal' size that they make most of their clothes for. This often excludes people who are a different shape and size to this limited 'ideal' and can result in negative feelings towards their appearance and in some cases body dysmorphia. It's important not to confuse sizing with fit. Our bodies are all uniquely shaped and we should not reduce our self-worth to the number on a clothes label. Accepting this can be liberating.

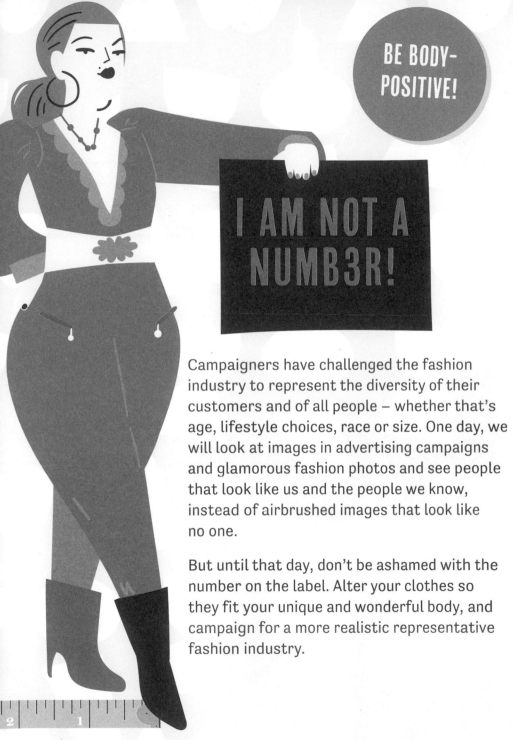

BE BODY-POSITIVE!

I AM NOT A NUMB3R!

Campaigners have challenged the fashion industry to represent the diversity of their customers and of all people – whether that's age, lifestyle choices, race or size. One day, we will look at images in advertising campaigns and glamorous fashion photos and see people that look like us and the people we know, instead of airbrushed images that look like no one.

But until that day, don't be ashamed with the number on the label. Alter your clothes so they fit your unique and wonderful body, and campaign for a more realistic representative fashion industry.

DO BUTTONS

One of the first key skills any mending activist will learn is to sew a button back on to a garment. Buttons can be made out of metal, glass, wood, plastic, ceramic, shell or even bone, so you can still make ethical choices about the ones you buy or choose to reuse. Why not creatively embellish a garment with buttons to add some colour, texture and interest to your clothes?

WHICH BUTTONS TO CHOOSE?

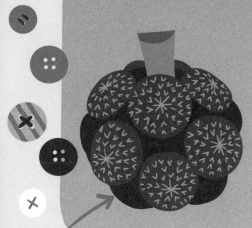

The best plant-based choices for buttons include bamboo, resin, and coconut shell. One of the latest ethical choices is *corozo* or *tagua*, found in Central and South America. Known as 'vegetable ivory', corozo is a type of resin made from the seed of a tropical palm tree and is extremely durable. Every button made from corozo is from a completely renewable resource with new seeds produced each season.

COROZO NUTS ARE SEEDS FROM THE TAGUA TREE.

Some fashion brands make their products difficult to repair and even omit a simple spare button, assuming (or hoping) their customers will throw the outfit in the bin if a button falls off and buy a whole new outfit instead! However, some brands are beginning to recognize their customers want to get the most out of the clothes they buy and offer a repair service.

How to sew a button on the right way

WHAT YOU WILL NEED:

 Button   Thread   Needle   Scissors

1 Thread the needle and tie a knot at the end of the thread.

2 Start at the back of the fabric. Push the needle up to the front and back down to create a stitch. Repeat to create a cross where the button will be.

3 With one hand holding the button in position, push the needle back up through the garment and through one hole of the button.

4 Push the needle back down through a different hole and the back of the fabric.

5 Repeat three or four times or until secure. Don't sew the button on *too* tightly as it will be hard to fasten.

6 Push the needle back through the hole in the button but not through the garment, so that it comes out underneath the button on the right side.

7 Wrap the thread around the thread that holds the button in place a few times before pushing the needle through the garment to the back.

8 Tie a knot to finish.

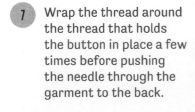

With a two- or four-hole button you can stitch straight across to make a _ or ═. For a four-hole you can also cross over to make an **x**.

DO HEMS

Want to make your trousers into shorts, or perhaps you find that your maxi skirt would look better as a midi? Altering the length of a garment by removing excess fabric is straightforward.

Turn-ups will allow you to shorten a pair of trousers without the commitment of cutting or sewing!

WHAT YOU WILL NEED:

- Tailor's chalk
- Thread
- Needle
- Scissors
- Iron
- Ruler
- Pins (or safety pins)

1. Put the item of clothing on inside out and play around with what length you would like it to be. Mark your chosen length with tailor's chalk.

2. Take the item off and lay it on a flat surface. Draw a line with a ruler and chalk where the marking is.

3. Add your hem allowance. This is 5cm below the original marking*. This is where you will cut. Draw a line with chalk, using the ruler to help you make sure it's the same size all the way around.

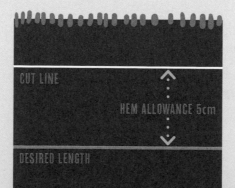

CUT LINE

HEM ALLOWANCE 5cm

DESIRED LENGTH

* This is a standard hem allowance. You can adjust it to whatever size you'd like.

4 Cut along the lowest chalk line and fold the hem allowance in half and half again to hide and enclose the cut edge to reach your desired length. Pin as you go. Be sure to fold towards the inside of the garment so the hem won't be seen.

5 Press the new hem with an iron before you sew it in place.

6 Pin to secure new hem. You may wish to tack the hem in place before sewing. A tack is a temporary running stitch in a contrasting thread.

7 Use a slip stitch to sew the hem in place, taking care to make the stitches small so you don't see them on the outside of the garment.

8 Remove the tacking stitch.

9 Pop them on and style accordingly.

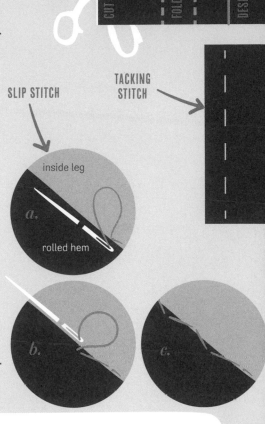

CUT LINE

FOLD LINES

DESIRED LENGTH

SLIP STITCH

TACKING STITCH

inside leg

a.

rolled hem

b.

c.

TOO SHORT?

Adding additional length to a garment can be done by unpicking a hem and making the new hem smaller. If there is not enough excess fabric in the hem then you may wish to add a strip of fabric or trim on the bottom of it to create more length or have no hem at all and leave the edge raw and frayed.

PART FOUR

New To You

Pre-loved, pre-owned, vintage and thrift are all terms to describe the same thing: second-hand! But there's no arguing that it's an incredibly affordable way to source clothes sustainably and responsibly. Trawling the rails of your local charity shop, vintage shop or scouring online resale sites is just as friendly to the planet as swapping and borrowing.

The global second-hand clothing market is huge and booming and you might be surprised by what others think of as 'rubbish'. Let's rewind back to our Wardrobe Workout (see page 24). What were the numerous reasons why you might have rejected some perfectly good clothes? Perhaps those garments were unwanted gifts, misguided purchases or clothes that simply no longer fit. Other people cast off their clothes for the same reasons, so one person's trash can literally be another person's treasure.

Charity shops provide an important service by stopping clothes from ending up in the bin and giving them the chance to be worn again. They also raise money for important causes. Some people have a problem with shopping in charity shops and second-hand clothes. They think that the clothes are dirty or that shopping this way is only for people who can't afford to buy new things.

This is far from the truth. Shopping second-hand means you can get designer brands at lower prices. Like a fast-fashion shopper, a charity shopper may be driven by the love of a bargain, but second-hand shoppers are also motivated by finding something unique, unusual and one of a kind.

In this section we'll show you how to shop second-hand and what to look out for when you buy. Find out how to avoid single-use fashion or a fashion faux pas with fake fur. Happy thrifting!

HOW TO SHOP SECOND-HAND

When shopping second-hand you'll be faced with jam-packed rails of potential treasures. The beauty of it is that you may find something from Primark hanging next to something from Prada. But rather than the name on the label, your shopping will become more about the cut, fabric and design of an item of clothing. Shopping second-hand will help you to take ownership of your own unique and individual style. Here are some tips on how to get the most out of it:

1 GIVE YOURSELF TIME

Give yourself enough time for trawling. Everything is one of a kind and will require your attention.

2 TRY BEFORE YOU BUY

Some clothes look better on the body so if the colour or print appeals try it on for size (unless you're buying online). Remember, sizing varies so if in doubt, try it on. Test different shapes and styles to help you understand what you like and what works for you. Would the garment work in an oversized style or benefit from some easy alterations? (See page 68.)

3 BE REALISTIC ABOUT REPAIRS

You may find the odd hole, missing button or dropped hem, and with your mending-activist skills, a repair might mean you're getting a bargain, especially if the item is marked down and 'sold as seen'. However, be realistic about undertaking big repair projects. How much are you able, or prepared, to do to alter the item?

④ FEEL THE FABRIC

Lots of clothes from the Sixties, Seventies and Eighties are made from synthetic materials. Give them a miss if you're prone to getting too hot, especially if it's a summer outfit. Avoid fabric covered in pilling (see page 27) – the fabric is likely to be poor quality or past its best. Look at the label, but also touch the fabric. Some fabrics are prone to cause static whilst others might be too see-through and impractical in certain lights. If in doubt, try it on.

Fashion often takes its inspiration from the past. Look out for original pieces from a decade that is inspiring current trends to get an authentic look.

⑤ CHECK FASTENINGS WORK

Stuck metal zips can be lubricated with some lip balm or bees wax. Missing buttons, hooks and eyes and poppers are easy to replace.

⑥ CHECK SEAMS

Seams are a big giveaway to whether something is well made. A French, flat-felled or bound seam is a sign of good quality – where the raw edge of the fabric has been tucked away.

⑦ SIGNS OF WEAR

Most worn-out clothes won't make the shop floor. Look out for items that might make fun alteration or refashioning projects (see page 78). Scuffed hems on trousers could be an opportunity for cropping or turning into shorts. Check collars, cuffs and armpits for discolouration (they might make a fun shibori project – see page 84). Check knitwear for signs of moth activity. If in doubt, freeze it for two weeks to kill any larvae.

FASHION ANIMAL

Some people argue that it's OK to wear the skin or fur of an animal if it's a vintage item in a charity shop because the animal has already been killed. Others will steer well clear, simply because it's made from a dead animal. You may come across older items in charity shops that are made from animals – whether or not you choose to buy them is a personal decision you can make when you know the facts behind the fashion.

TO FUR OR FAUX FUR?

Fur fell out of fashion favour in the 1990s, but it has never truly disappeared, especially in second-hand shops. The pro-fur argument stipulates that it is a sustainable and natural fibre that biodegrades, unlike the chemical man-made substitute (often acrylic or nylon) that may take upwards of 600 years to degrade. However, real fur requires formaldehyde and chromium to stop it rotting. Some people argue that fake fur normalizes the increasing demand for real fur, and others claim it is a by-product of the food industry, which is incredibly hard to prove or disprove. Animal-rights campaigners reveal films and photos of fur-farm production that beg the question: is it ever humane to kill an animal for its skin?

SUFFERING SNAKES

Whether you're a lover of snakes or not, the process of turning them into a pair of boots or a bag is enough to make your stomach churn. If the snakes were cute and cuddly would we be more appalled by their treatment? Although some snakes are grown in controlled environments, a lot of them are also removed from the wild. It is said that hunting wild snakes (a natural predator) has led to growing numbers of rats.

LONG LIVE LEATHER?

Leather is classic, timeless and hard-wearing, and it's easy to forget it is an animal product. Cows are the most farmed animal on the planet. Tanneries process cows' skin before it is made into leather bags and shoes. Some 400 tanneries on the banks of India's holy river Ganges spew out a cocktail of toxic chemicals, such as manganese, lead, copper and chromium. Not only are these chemicals and heavy metals killing the river, but they are carcinogenic (can cause cancer). These chemicals run off into the ground, polluting the drinking water and crops that enter the human food chain. Vegetable tanning is a more traditional process which doesn't use these toxic chemicals but it is time-consuming and therefore more costly.

Crocodile Crazy

Crocodile skin has long been associated with luxury fashion, and by the 1930s, crocodile products were being mass-produced. Between 1954 and 1970, two to three million skins were being sold each year. Numbers declined, which led to conservation laws being introduced to protect crocodiles from hunters. Undeterred, the luxury fashion market took to taking crocodile eggs from the wild and raising them in farms to then be slaughtered at three years old when their bellies reach the correct size.

Up to four crocodiles are needed to make a Hermès Birkin bag, currently priced at £140,000.

SINGLE-USE FASHION

In recent years, we've become increasingly aware that single-use plastics, such as bags, drinks bottles and plastic straws, wreak havoc on our planet. We see shocking images of these everyday disposable items washed up on beaches and littering our environment once they've served their purpose, and we can no longer use them. Yet single-use can also apply to the clothes we wear. Some clothes are designed to be used only once.

ACCESSORIZE

HERE ARE SOME COMMON SINGLE-USE ITEMS:

- Prom dress
- Wedding dress
- Fancy-dress costume
- Christmas jumper
- Event T-shirt
- Shoe covers
- Latex gloves
- Pedicure slippers

You can easily create a fancy-dress outfit without it damaging your pocket or the earth.

FASHION LIBRARIAN

Hiring clothes for special occasions is not a new idea. However, renting clothes from fashion libraries is becoming increasingly popular. It works by paying a subscription fee but never owning the clothes.

Rather than buying something new, renting means you can use a garment for a set period of time before returning it and renting something else.

Fancy fashion

It's unlikely you'll wear a fancy-dress costume more than once. Avoid falling at this single-use hurdle and follow these top tips for getting your fancy-dress costume right without you or the planet paying the price.

SOURCE AT HOME

STYLE HAIR AND MAKE-UP

CUSTOMIZE

DO YOUR RESEARCH

Collect ideas and images around the theme or character you are looking to dress up as.

GET CREATIVE WITH WHAT YOU HAVE

Have you got something at home that can form the basis of your fancy-dress outfit? Take a look in your wardrobe and see if you can style it up with accessories, hair and make-up. If you've got old bed sheets or blankets they can be used as a great source of fabric – they make great superhero capes! Open your eyes to everyday objects around the house, too. Velcro and safety pins can work as temporary solutions to refashion something you have without permanently altering it.

ASK AROUND

See if someone you know has something you can borrow for the occasion. You might be surprised to find a friend has a wig or a hat that will complete your costume without the stress of buying something and knowing you'll be unlikely to wear it again.

SOURCE SECOND-HAND

Shop second-hand with your fancy-dress costume in mind. And don't forget you can donate it back to charity when you no longer need it . . . .

If recycling is using something again, upcycling is making it even better than it was before!

PASSION FOR REFASHION

Refashioning or upcycling is an opportunity to turn old clothes into something new and exciting. It adds value to what might be seen as waste or rubbish and can lead to surprising results.

Home-sewing enthusiasts and some emerging designers have experimented with refashioning as a way to use up textile waste. Upcycling existing clothes is incredibly difficult to do in big quantities, because each individual item to be upcycled will be made slightly differently. This means production is slower and more costly compared with mass-produced clothes found on the high street. But with refashioning and upcycling each piece is likely to be unique so you'll know you won't bump into someone wearing the same thing as you. It also saves clothes from landfill or incineration.

SURPLUS TO REQUIREMENTS

Some designers use 'end of roll' or reclaimed surplus fabrics in their collections. This is not strictly upcycling because these fabrics were never used, but they are a symptom of over-production which is a common problem in the fashion world. You could argue that taking these fabrics from larger fashion brands allows them to continue over-ordering.

Here is a 'jeanius' refashioning idea to get you started:

Sleeveless Jean Jacket

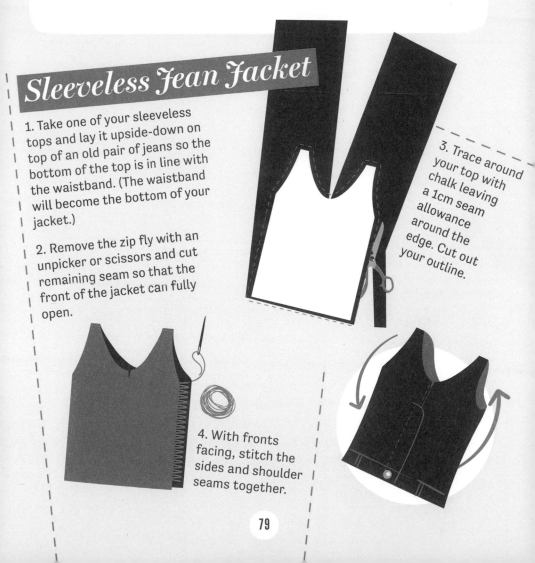

1. Take one of your sleeveless tops and lay it upside-down on top of an old pair of jeans so the bottom of the top is in line with the waistband. (The waistband will become the bottom of your jacket.)

2. Remove the zip fly with an unpicker or scissors and cut remaining seam so that the front of the jacket can fully open.

3. Trace around your top with chalk leaving a 1cm seam allowance around the edge. Cut out your outline.

4. With fronts facing, stitch the sides and shoulder seams together.

DO STAINS

Even if a stain turns out to be permanent, this doesn't mean the end of a piece of clothing. Instead, see it as an opportunity for creative customization and experiment! Be as bold as you like, and go to town with your design, trying out some of the cover-up techniques shown here.

Stains can be a pain, especially if left untreated. The treatment is all about chemistry. Activate your inner chemist by matching the common household ingredient with the type of stain from our guide below . . .

THE SCIENCE BIT:

If a stain is fresh, blot it with tissue or run under cold water (hot water will seal the stain), then get to work with the right spot treatment:

Ballpoint pen – rub with vinegar, soap or hairspray, or soak in milk.

Blood – rub with bicarbonate of soda, vinegar, cornstarch or soak in saltwater.

Candle wax – scrape off or iron stain over a piece of paper.

Chewing gum – freeze or use an ice cube to harden, then scrape off.

Coffee – soak with lukewarm water then wash.

Mud – dry out, brush off, then wash.

Sweat marks – rub with bicarbonate of soda, vinegar or lemon juice.

Oil – rub with washing-up liquid or shampoo.

APPLY APPLIQUÉ

Appliqué is the process of taking one fabric and attaching it on top of another to form a picture or pattern. Take a contrasting fabric and use a paper template or draw your desired shape freestyle straight on to the fabric, using tailor's chalk. Then cut it out. Place the fabric shape on to the garment and pin and tack (see page 52) into position. Alternatively, you can use a temporary iron-on adhesive if the fabric has a high melting point (check instructions and be careful with iron settings on some synthetic fabrics). Stitch around the outside of the shape to attach it and cover up the stain. A blanket or whip stitch is good here to stop the edge of the fabric fraying (see page 53). Remove pins and tacks. Voilà!

For a quick and easy fix, colour in the stains using fabric pens. Be as bold or as decorative as you like.

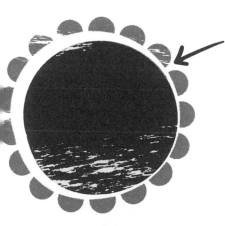

BLOCK OR LINO PRINT

Whether you're a fan of bold geometric shapes or fine intricate patterns, printing on to your garment to cover up a stain is a great option to bring it back to life. You don't even need fancy tools for this, as a knife and potato works just as well as carving your design into wood, rubber, foam or linoleum – just be careful when cutting. Cut or carve your desired design into the material you have chosen. Then print on to the garment using fabric paint (make sure you get one that is suitable for the type of fabric). You may consider repeating the design so it becomes a pattern that covers the garment not just the stain.

Can't get it out or cover it up? Head over to page 84 for shibori dyeing tips.

DO NATURAL DYES

Natural dyes are a great, non-toxic way of reviving old clothes and covering up stains. Dating back to Neolithic times, natural dyes were used worldwide before synthetic chemical dyes were discovered in the late 19th century. Now 20 per cent of global industrial water pollution comes from treating and dyeing textiles. Natural dyeing can often give surprising results so experiment and see what colours you can create with nature's bounty.

WHAT YOU WILL NEED:

- Old heatproof pan
- Fabric*
- Natural-dye raw materials
- A mordant or fixative, such as alum, saltwater (ratio 16:1 – 16 parts water to one part salt) or vinegar water (ratio 4:1 – four parts water to one part vinegar)**
- Wooden spoon or stick
- Water
- Protective gloves and mask
- Knife
- Wooden spoon

** A 'part' can be any unit measurement you choose e.g. if one part is 100ml and the ratio for vinegar water is 4:1, use 400ml water combined with 100ml vinegar.

*Dyes work best on plant- or protein-based fibres (or fabrics with more than 50 per cent natural fibres). Do a test on the same or similar fabric before dyeing the real thing so you get an idea of the strength of colour. Keep a notebook to record your successes and failures for future dyeing projects.

Be safe!
Wear a protective mask and gloves, and work in a well-ventilated area. Take care when heating the dye bath, and use old pans and equipment that will not be used for preparing food.

1

PREPARE FABRIC

Ensure fabric is clean. New fabric should be pre-washed and dried to allow for shrinkage. Prepare the fabric with your mordant or fixative. This ensures the dye fixes to the fabric otherwise it will fade and wash out!

2

PREPARE DYE BATH

Cut raw materials into small pieces and place in pan with water. (Use one part raw material to two parts water.) Heat to near boiling but DO NOT BOIL (this can ruin some raw materials). Simmer for an hour or until colour deepens. This is a good time to test the fabric. When happy with the colour, remove or strain the raw materials.

3

DYE FABRIC

Place fabric into dye bath. Simmer gently for 30 minutes. When happy with the colour, remove fabric with spoon. Cool down, wring and hang to dry.

RAW INGREDIENTS:

Natural dyes are mainly derived from animal, insects, plants or fungi. Here are some easily found ingredients for natural dyeing that you may find in your home, compost bin, garden or local surroundings.

ONION SKIN
for yellows and purples

TURMERIC ROOT OR POWDER
for vibrant yellow

MADDER ROOT
for vivid reds

RED CABBAGE
for shades of blue

HIBISCUS FLOWERS
for reds and purples

POMEGRANATE
for yellows and oranges

BERRIES AND AVOCADO PITS
for pinks

CHAMOMILE AND MARIGOLD
for shades of yellow

INDIGO
for vivid blues

DO SHIBORI

Shibori is an ancient Japanese dyeing technique that involves manipulating fabric so that areas of it resist the dye to create shapes and patterns. Fabric can be folded, twisted, tied, pressed, clamped, bound and sewn before it is dipped into a dye bath. Batik, which uses wax as a 'resist' to create patterns, and tie dye, made popular by hippies in the 1960s, are other forms of resist dyeing. The beauty of shibori is it can be difficult to predict the end result. The type of fabric, texture, dye and how you choose to manipulate the fabric will create unique patterns.

Itajame

Itajame is a form of shibori which uses clamps to resist the dye. You could make your own clamps with different-shaped pieces of wood and screws, or alternatively use clothes pegs. Fold fabric into squares, triangles or wedges. The combination of how the clamps are arranged along with the way the fabric has been folded creates resistance to the dye and a host of amazing patterns.

WHAT YOU WILL NEED:

- Clamps in rectangles, circles, triangles or squares. Or you can use pegs or clips.
- Protective gloves and apron
- Pre-made dye bath
- Water

1

MANIPULATE

your pre-washed fabric by folding the fabric and placing a clamp or peg.

2

DIP

some of the fabric, all of the fabric or dip dye (pull the garment in and out of the water) to create a graded fade.

3

OXIDIZE

(get oxygen into) the fabric to help the dye develop. You can do this by unfolding the fabric to get air to it or by running the dyed fabric under clean running water.

4

REPEAT

dyeing and oxidizing until happy with colour. Remove clamps and rinse under cold or warm water.

5

HANG DRY

Try one of these patterns or experiment with your own.

6

WASH

fabric in machine with gentle detergent.

Folding and clamping the cloth in different ways gives you different patterns.

PART FIVE

New New

You've spring-cleaned your wardrobe and are left with a good selection of clothes, uncovered some gems and perhaps even experimented with some new styles. You might have been inspired to take part in some clothes swapping, sold a few pieces online and explored the magic of second-hand shopping. Those clothes that weren't quite working for you have been gloriously refashioned or tenderly repaired, but you have reached a point where you need to buy something new. Now your sustainable-fashion journey will begin to navigate the world of new clothes . . .

Around 100 billion new clothes are produced globally every year. How do you reconcile your own personal values – caring for the planet, the impact on human life, the rights of animals – with the vast array of clothing choices out there? Which fabrics are best? Is organic better than Fairtrade? How can you guarantee that people haven't been exploited to produce the clothes you buy? Should you boycott a particular brand for bad eco-practice?

Understanding what to look out for so you can shop with an ethical mind is simply a case of educating yourself. If you are aware of the problems and open to being part of the solutions . . .

YOU CAN DEMAND A BETTER, FAIRER FASHION INDUSTRY THAT PUTS PEOPLE AND PLANET FIRST.

This section will explore some of the key issues surrounding the fashion industry today, from the human-rights issues involved in the making of a cotton T-shirt to exciting innovations in zero-waste manufacturing, alternative fabrics and fashion activism. Not only will you be armed with the information you'll need to become a more mindful shopper, but you can even consider a career in the fashion industry where you could make a hands-on difference.

THE REAL COST

Let's go back to the life cycle of our T-shirt and take a look at the real cost behind all the stages of its journey into your wardrobe.

Imagine each stage in the process shown on page 12 is one job that someone does in the supply chain (there are many more, but let's keep it simple for now!). Think about what each job may involve and how much time and skill it might take.

Let's say that you bought the T-shirt for £5. Now think about distributing the £5 amongst the people that made the T-shirt. It doesn't stretch very far, does it? The shop you bought it from will also need to pay rent and bills in addition to wanting to make a decent profit on the sale of each T-shirt.

The solution is not quite as simple as us, the consumer, paying more for something. A high price tag does not guarantee clothes are made ethically and workers are paid a living wage . . . because the priority of fashion brands is to make a profit for their shareholders.

A cotton T-shirt might seem like an ethical choice for a conscious consumer but its relatively low price comes with its own issues for the humans and countries involved in its production.

The mass production of cotton has a long and problematic history. In the 19th century, the global trade in cotton exploded, and it relied heavily on the enslavement of African people in the United States. The popularity of cotton made it the first mass-produced fabric to be traded globally, and it had a devastating effect on millions of African lives.

Even now, forms of modern cotton slavery exist with some brands pledging not to source Uzbek cotton. This is due to the Uzbekistan government forcing hundreds of thousands of ordinary people every year to pick cotton during the harvest season. However, it is sometimes difficult to trace the cotton back to its source and some brands may still unknowingly be using it.

A Bangladeshi garment worker will earn an average of £73 per month.

The CEO of a fashion brand will earn in their **lunch break** what a garment worker earns in an **entire year**.

WHITE GOLD

A whopping 50 per cent of all clothes in the world are made from cotton. It's an incredibly versatile natural fibre, and it can appear under different names depending on how the fibre is knitted or woven. Twill, poplin, corduroy, cotton jersey, muslin and denim are all types of cotton with different qualities, and there are many more. But it might surprise you to know that cotton is an incredibly thirsty plant which is often grown in hot countries, such as India, where water is scarce . . . .

Back to our T-shirt: we produce 2.4 billion new T-shirts globally every year. Just one of them can use up to 2,700 litres of water, depending on where and how it's grown. Water is integral to the survival of humanity and life on earth and the average adult needs to drink around two litres a day. But only one per cent of the water in the world is suitable for human consumption.

CAN YOU IMAGINE HOW MANY YEARS WORTH OF DRINKING WATER ARE REPRESENTED BY THE COTTON ITEMS IN YOUR WARDROBE?

India is one of the world's largest exporters of cotton. The water consumed to grow its cotton exports is enough to supply 85 per cent of the country's 1.24 billion people with 100 litres of water every day for a year. However, more than 100 million people in India do not have access to safe water.

India's rate of water consumption for cotton growth is far higher than in the rest of the world because it does not have a system for reducing it. There is also a far higher rate of water pollution in India, with 50 per cent of all its pesticides used as part of the cotton-growing process.

India currently produces two thirds of the world's organic cotton – which has a lower net water use because it uses no chemicals. However, this is just two per cent of the country's cotton output

The global pharmaceutical company Bayer produce chemical pesticides and fertilizers. They currently have a 95 per cent monopoly of the cotton-seed market in India. This makes it difficult for farmers to acquire organic non-genetically modified seeds to grow cotton with less water and fewer chemicals.

What happened to the Aral Sea?

In Central Asia the Aral Sea is the fourth largest inland lake, situated in between Uzbekistan and Kazakhstan. It was a giant 68,000 square kilometres in size. In the 1950s, the Soviet Union diverted the freshwater rivers that were feeding the Aral Sea to irrigate surrounding cotton fields. What was once a thriving fishing village is now a salty desert because of the unsustainable, industrial scale of the cotton-growing. Only ten per cent of the Aral Sea remains today.

PESKY PESTICIDES

The rise of cheap cotton has led to more intensive industrial farming. But pests and insects love cotton, and they can spell disaster for a farmer's crop. To protect their cotton, conventional farmers have become increasingly reliant on chemical fertilizers and pesticides to destroy any pests that may cause damage to the plant. In addition, two thirds of cotton seeds used around the world are now genetically modified (GM) requiring more and more chemical fertilizers and pesticides to protect them.

These chemicals are disrupting fragile ecosystems and damaging the health of people that work on cotton farms. Blanket-spraying chemicals over cotton fields does not target and kill only one insect or pest; it kills or harms all of them, even the 'good' ones. Chemicals in the soil run off into the water systems contaminating local water supplies. People who work in the cotton fields, and those living nearby, come into contact with these toxic pesticides. They have even been linked to severe health problems, such as cancers, neurological diseases and even death.

YES TO
ORGANIC
FARMING

GO ORGANIC

The organic food we see in our supermarkets essentially ensures that no harmful chemical pesticides or fertilizers have been used. This can also apply to the clothes we wear. Organic farming uses traditional farming approaches that work with, and not against, the natural world. Farmers rotate crops and let fields rest (in what are called fallow years) to ensure vital nutrients are returned to the soil after growing cotton. This removes the reliance on chemical fertilizers.

Understanding and identifying the pests that do damage, and those that don't, is an important part of the process. Growing plants such as cashew nuts nearby can help to attract harmful pests away from cotton fields and towards plants that they do not damage. Farmers can use plants, such as neem, to make a natural insect-repellent spray.

Organic cotton has the added benefit of using less water, supplying a better wage for cotton farmers as well as improving worker health and the health of the environment. Organic cotton is becoming increasingly popular as brands react to consumer demand, but it currently accounts for only one per cent of all cotton production. It takes three years for a conventional cotton farmer to convert to organic farming and they must conform to strict standards for external certifications that cost money, adding to the overall price. Look out for official organic certifications when buying new, such as Global Organic Textile Standard (GOTS) and the Organic Content Standard (OCS).

THE MAGIC OF HEMP

Hemp is one of the first plants to have been spun into usable fibres over 10,000 years ago. It's one of the most versatile plants: it can be grown in most climates and turned into paper, rope, textiles, clothing, biodegradable plastics, paint, insulation, food and animal feed. But the magic of hemp doesn't just stop there. It grows rapidly, requires very little water (compared to cotton), uses little to no chemical pesticides, is incredibly resilient and actually removes toxins from the soil and air.

Despite hemp's versatility, it has fallen in and out of fashion over the years. King Henry VIII was a big fan and he passed an act that fined farmers who refused to grow it. It was a popular choice of material on naval ships where it was used for sails and ropes. In the United States, presidents George Washington and Thomas Jefferson both cultivated it and yet in both Europe and the United States, hemp has been subject to restrictions, strict licencing and even been made illegal.

But why? One theory is that during the 1930s, US newspaper magnate Randolph Hearst used his power and influence to campaign against hemp. He had invested in wood pulp and cotton-seed oil and would benefit greatly if hemp was made illegal. Lobbying from paper, timber and chemical companies persuaded the US government to ban hemp production in 1937. The ban coincided with the invention of the synthetic fabric nylon.

The first Levi jeans were made out of hemp.

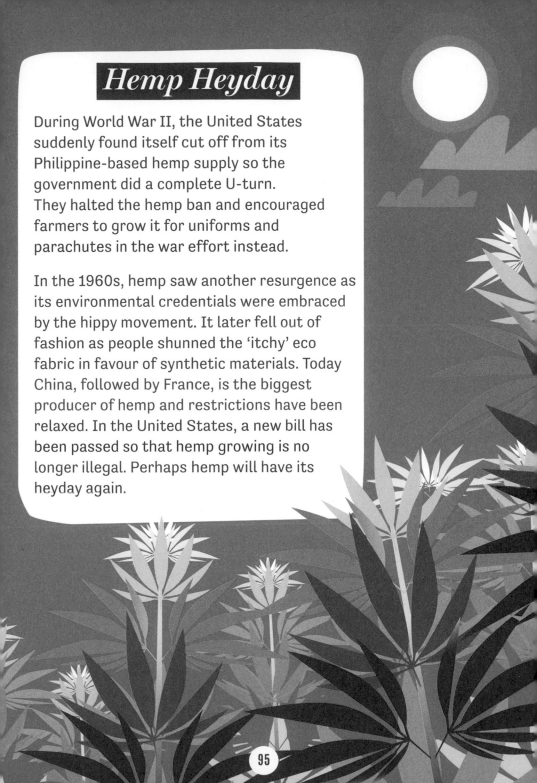

Hemp Heyday

During World War II, the United States suddenly found itself cut off from its Philippine-based hemp supply so the government did a complete U-turn. They halted the hemp ban and encouraged farmers to grow it for uniforms and parachutes in the war effort instead.

In the 1960s, hemp saw another resurgence as its environmental credentials were embraced by the hippy movement. It later fell out of fashion as people shunned the 'itchy' eco fabric in favour of synthetic materials. Today China, followed by France, is the biggest producer of hemp and restrictions have been relaxed. In the United States, a new bill has been passed so that hemp growing is no longer illegal. Perhaps hemp will have its heyday again.

ARE JEANS ETHICAL?

On any given day, it's estimated that 50 per cent of the world's population are wearing denim jeans, making it a choice worn and loved by all. If this wardrobe staple has been designed to last a long time it might seem to be an ethical choice, but in reality, they might not be quite as sustainable as they seem.

MATERIAL MATTERS

Denim jeans are commonly made out of cotton which we know is a thirsty plant that (unless organic) requires huge amounts of chemical fertilizers and pesticides. It's estimated to take more than 8,000 litres of water to produce the cotton needed to make one pair of jeans. That's equivalent to about 100 baths!

Modern jeans often have some stretch which means the cotton has been blended with a synthetic material such as Lycra or elastane. This mixed fibre is currently impossible to recycle without negative repercussions on our environment. Levi's have been working on technology to process hemp as a substitute for cotton, a durable fibre that grows abundantly with less intervention (see page 94).

WELL WORN

Jeans were the hard-wearing uniform of US workers and cowboys. Developed in 1873 by Levi Strauss and tailor Jacob Davis, the metal studs and reinforced stitching ensured they were designed to be strong and durable and could be worn in tough working conditions.

Well-worn jeans develop a distinctive patina as they fade and rip. Many fashion brands manufacture this look so the jeans appear tired and distressed before anyone has even worn them. Acid wash, stonewash and sandblasting are common processes used to achieve this look. The process of sandblasting involves firing sand through a high-powered hose to wear away the surface of the jeans. It has been linked to the deadly lung disease silicosis among workers who may not have access to protective masks and clothing. Any of these processes shorten the life of the fabric by weakening it. Luckily there are other ways we can make our clothes look like they're falling apart. We can wear them a lot instead!

WONDERFUL WOOL

The versatility of wool is undeniable. Whether it's knitted or woven, it provides great insulation, is water-repellent, UV-resistant and is really easy to dye. Not to mention it is incredibly durable. Yet wool, with its long list of positive attributes, sits in the shadow of synthetic fabrics and represents less than two per cent of all fibres consumed.

As a natural and biodegradable fibre, wool has lots of properties that get the ethical thumbs up. It's self-cleaning, anti-bacterial and stain- and wrinkle-resistant, which means that if you're not a fan of washing, wear wool! Its ability to resist bad smells, unlike synthetic fabrics, could make it a far better choice of fabric for sportswear. Especially as it's a breathable fibre that can keep you cool if you're hot and warm if you're cold, which might explain why it's suitable for wearing in most climates.

Depending on climate, access to shelter and the type of animal and breed, farmers will shear animals, such as sheep, goats, llamas and alpacas, once or possibly a few times a year to remove their hair. It is claimed that this is done so that the animals won't overheat in the summer months, or in some instances attract insects and disease. The hair, or wool, is therefore a renewable by-product as the animal will produce more hair and so the cycle continues.

In 2010, the global initiative Campaign for Wool was launched to increase awareness of the benefits of wool, to work with farmers, manufacturers and designers and increase demand for wool internationally.

IS WOOL ETHICAL?

Some animal-rights campaigners argue that animals are selectively bred to grow more wool, meaning they have to be sheared. Where wild breeds will have just enough wool to protect them, this is not the case for domestic breeds, such as merino sheep, who grow too much so that humans can use it.

Humans have been selectively breeding plants and animals in this way for hundreds of thousands of years, but animal-rights campaigners state that this human intervention is a form of cruelty. Pro-wool campaigners will argue that it's more cruel for humans not to shear sheep because they could overheat and become immobile.

There is also the problem with shearing itself. On some large-scale industrial farms, shearers are reported to be paid per sheep rather than by the hour, encouraging them to work quickly and ruthlessly, causing harm and injury to the animals in the process. It would be unfair to claim that this is the case for all farms as working conditions vary country to country and farm to farm.

MULESING

Sheep are prone to the fatal condition flystrike. Mulesing is a controversial surgical procedure that involves removing the folds of skin off the sheep's hindquarters to prevent flies laying eggs there. In Australia, some farmers believe mulesing to be essential, arguing that not doing it can lead to a long, painful death for the sheep. Protests from consumers and campaigners have led to some brands boycotting wool supplies from farms that carry out this practice, whilst in New Zealand legislation banning mulesing came into effect in 2018. Selectively breeding animals with fewer wrinkles has been cited as a possible solution.

As with all industrial animal-rearing, there is also an environmental cost. It is well known that livestock emit methane gas, a greenhouse gas, into the atmosphere. But desertification, topsoil loss and even deforestation caused by overgrazing are also concerns. Some research suggests that if sheep flocks are well-managed they can provide much-needed nutrients to the soil that can help absorb carbon dioxide, another greenhouse gas.

The only alternatives to wool currently offered by fashion brands are synthetic fibres, such as acrylic or polyester blends, but these come with their own problems (see page 108). These synthetic non-renewable fibres have negative impacts on the planet and are prone to shedding micro-plastics during washing, threatening marine life and damaging our water systems.

The question of whether or not you should wear wool is complex and nuanced. All you can do is get informed and make the right choice for your own values and belief system.

PLASTIC FANTASTIC?

Look through the care labels in your wardrobe. Unless you exclusively buy natural fabrics, you'll probably find there's a melting pot of acetates, polyamide, elastane, rayon, nylon and polyester in there. You may be surprised to find that some of your clothing mixes natural and synthetic fibres.

There are two types of synthetic fabrics: those made from chemically treating cellulose from natural renewable sources, such as wood pulp, and those engineered from oil refinery by-products. The former has been around since the 19th century when the first artificial silk was created from cellulose using a chemical process. Since the 1940s, fabrics have been made from synthesizing oil leftover from car and plane fossil-fuel refining. The best known are nylon, polyester and PVC.

SYNTHETIC SIXTIES

In the 1960s, 'plastic fashion' boomed as designers looked to new technologies and materials, and to the future. The British fashion designer Mary Quant was the first to experiment with PVC for rainwear, while in France, Pierre Cardin created the iconic space-age looks commonly associated with the decade.

IS VISCOSE ETHICAL?

Viscose is the oldest manufactured fibre, first being produced in 1883 as a silk alternative. Viscose (a type of rayon) is made from wood pulp, which goes through several chemical and manufacturing processes to make fabric.

Because viscose is made from plants, it is often cited as being environmentally friendly and sustainable. But is it?

To make viscose, and make it durable, it must be chemically treated. The recycled wood pulp is treated with chemicals such as ammonia, acetone, caustic soda and sulphuric acid. This is a fabric which comes from a natural and sustainable source but is made with chemicals.

Viscose is increasingly being manufactured using the **Lyocell process**. This method produces little waste product, making it far more eco-friendly.

Today, over half of all fibres are synthetic and 35 million tonnes of synthetic materials are produced globally. A manufacturer of polyester may say that the fabric is extremely durable, quick to dry and cheap to produce. However, it takes a long time to degrade, even if it lasts in the wardrobe for a long time (see page 34). We also know that every time fabrics, such as polyester, are washed they release tiny plastic microfibres (see page 108) into the planet's water supply.

All fabrics used to make clothes come from our natural world, but the way these raw materials are extracted, processed (synthesized) and manufactured have an impact on people and our planet. However, when it comes to weighing up whether natural or synthetic fabrics are more ethical, it's not quite so black and white. You can weigh up some of the pros and cons of each one by checking clothing labels, doing your research and then using our guide on p106 to decode your fabric choices.

There are four key things to consider when choosing a garment:

1
IS IT DURABLE?

The best way to judge a fabric is to touch it. If it feels soft, substantial and contains longer fibres, then it is likely to be stronger and last longer. Consider whether it will wash and wear well. Early signs of pilling, flaking, thinning, fading and losing shape indicate low quality. But even if the fabric is durable, if a garment is poorly constructed it can still fall apart.

Best to choose: leather, polyester, bast, metal, natural polymers

2
HOW MUCH WATER HAS IT USED?

Water is used in the production of all materials but some notable fabrics use less than others. Remember that our simple white cotton T-shirt can use up to 2,700 litres of water, and it can take about 10,000 litres of water to produce one kilogram of cotton fabric.

Best to choose: Bast

IS IT RENEWABLE AND SUSTAINABLE?

The resources required to make textiles – water, land and energy – are not finite, and you will need to check if renewable resources were used in the making of your garment. Forest clearance is a huge issue so look out for sustainably and responsibly sourced certifications such as from the Forest Stewardship Council (FSC). Look out for clothes made from recycled renewable materials. Fashion is responsible for eight per cent of the global climate impact from carbon dioxide production and cotton is responsible for 18 per cent of global pesticide use. Make sure your choice of fabric is as sustainable as possible.

Best to choose: animal hairs (not skin!), bast, leaf, seed hair, fruit, natural polymers (viscose rayon, lyocell, bamboo, acetate, modal)

4

IS IT BIODEGRADABLE?

What happens to the fabric at the end of its life? Does it biodegrade? Remember that certain fastenings and finishings won't degrade, such as metal zips, plastic buttons and polyester thread used to sew the garment together.

Best to choose: rubber (natural not synthetic), bast, seed hair, leaf, fruit, protein

The fashion industry accounts for more than **8% of global climate impact**, which is greater than all international flights and sea shipping combined.

THE FIBRE FAMILY TREE

Know where your fabrics come from with this at-a-glance guide . . .

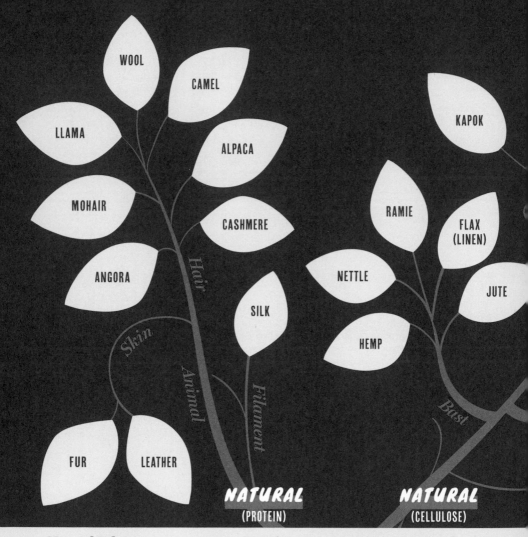

WOOL

CAMEL

KAPOK

LLAMA

ALPACA

MOHAIR

RAMIE

FLAX
(LINEN)

CASHMERE

ANGORA

NETTLE

JUTE

SILK

HEMP

Hair

Skin

Animal

Filament

Bast

FUR

LEATHER

NATURAL
(PROTEIN)

NATURAL
(CELLULOSE)

Natural Polymer
Naturally occurring fibres consisting of long molecules strung together. Also known as regenerative or manufactured.

Protein
Fibres taken from an animal.

Cellulose
Fibres made from plant cell walls.

Natural
Fibres that exist in nature.

Filament
A continuous long fibre. Silk is the only natural filament.

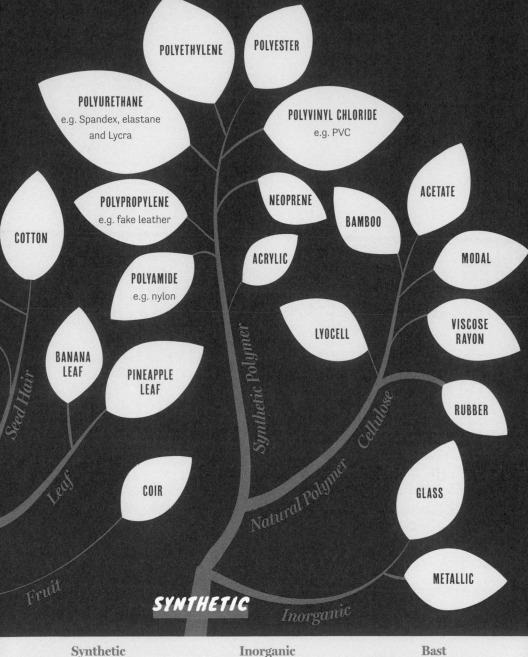

POLYETHYLENE

POLYESTER

POLYURETHANE
e.g. Spandex, elastane and Lycra

POLYVINYL CHLORIDE
e.g. PVC

ACETATE

POLYPROPYLENE
e.g. fake leather

NEOPRENE

BAMBOO

COTTON

ACRYLIC

MODAL

POLYAMIDE
e.g. nylon

LYOCELL

VISCOSE
RAYON

BANANA
LEAF

PINEAPPLE
LEAF

RUBBER

Seed Hair

Synthetic Polymer

Cellulose

COIR

GLASS

Leaf

Natural Polymer

Fruit

SYNTHETIC

METALLIC

Inorganic

Synthetic
Man-made fibres that are manufactured in factories using chemical synthesis.

Inorganic
A man-made material not derived from plants or animals, such as rocks, minerals and metals.

Bast
The fibrous material inside plants and trees, between the outer layer and core.

Synthetic Polymer
Fibres manufactured as a by-product of petroleum oil.

MICROFIBRE MADNESS

Around two thirds of the clothes we wear today contain synthetic fibres such as polyester. Why is this a problem? Plastic! It's estimated that the fashion industry is responsible for one third of all the plastic pollution in the ocean – and synthetic materials are at the centre of this environmental disaster. Every time a synthetic garment is washed in a machine it sheds an estimated 700,000 tiny plastic microfibres, according to environmental organization, Greenpeace. That's every time, every wash.

Synthetic fabrics tend to trap smells, which means we wash clothes made from these fibres more often. The plastic microfibres are less than 5mm long and thinner than a human hair. They make their way through the filters of the washing machine into our water systems and eventually reach the oceans, posing a threat to marine life. Plastic microfibres have even been found in seafood sold to humans to eat.

We need everyone from fashion brands and washing-machine manufacturers to water companies to come up with a way of tackling this issue but this could take some time. What action can you take right now? It's simple: wash your clothes less often.

Washing your clothes less may sound gross but it's a good strategy for softening your impact on the planet – reducing everything from energy use to the amount of microfibres released into our oceans.

Washing and drying a five kilogram load of washing every two days creates nearly 440 kilograms of carbon dioxide emissions in a year, mostly from the drying. You can try to dry your clothes naturally, ideally outside.

WASH LESS . . .

- Air clothes in between wears so you can wear them again.

- If you have pets, use a clothes brush or wrap sticky tape around your hand to remove pet hair.

- Spot wash instead of washing the whole item.

WASH SMARTER . . .

- Wash at 30°C* and on shorter cycles to reduce energy and carbon dioxide emissions.

- Make sure the washing machine is full.

- Dry clothes outside.

* Scientists are currently debating whether low temperature washing releases more microfibres.

Do Stains!
see page 80

Future Fashion

It's impossible to ignore fashion's impact on the environment. There is a sense of urgency to change the way we produce, consume and dispose of clothes if we're to protect our shared home. We know that most of our clothes come from animals, plants or fossil fuels, but we cannot keep using more and more new raw natural materials. We shouldn't be pumping toxic chemicals into the land and water supplies of communities. We certainly cannot keep burning clothes, or burying the problem that there are simply too many clothes that we can usefully use. We must not continue exploiting people living in poverty who work for long hours and low pay to make our clothes.

With this heightened sense of environmental and social consciousness there is a desire for a shake-up. We all have a responsibility to protect the future of our planet and fashion needs to lead this change. Firstly the fashion industry needs to be transparent so that it can see and understand the problems it needs to fix. The fashion industry needs to be honest so that we can be sure we share the same values and philosophies. As conscious consumers, we need to trust that our decisions are based on clear and freely available information.

The fashion industry also needs to take responsibility for the waste it creates by producing less stuff and ensuring that what is produced can be properly recycled. The industry needs to lead innovation and new technology but not to make us buy more stuff we don't need. We need to see clothes production use less precious water, fewer harmful chemicals and be zero waste because recycling is good, but not good enough.

The fashion industry that employs so many people around the world needs to respect these people and provide them with a safe working environment and a decent living wage.

We need a more ethical and sustainable fashion industry, and we need to create this together. As conscious consumers and active citizens, we can put pressure on brands and put our money where our hearts are. But it's not as simple as buying our way out of this problem. Sustainability is avoiding the depletion of natural resources in order to maintain an ecological balance so we can ensure that what we have and use today will also be available for future generations.

BUT THE BIG QUESTION IS . . .

CAN FASHION EVER BE SUSTAINABLE?

ALTERNATIVE FABRICS

Fashion has become increasingly reliant on fossil-fuel based materials such as polyester and nylon, which we know have negative environmental impacts. However, in terms of alternatives, it's certainly not as clear-cut as choosing natural fabrics over synthetic ones, especially once we've factored in issues such as deforestation, water scarcity, toxic chemicals and animal welfare. It's obvious that there is a demand for something new and different.

Sustainability is driving innovations to create alternative fabrics, but this requires collaboration and cooperation from fashion brands to share research and information. By working together towards a collective goal, it might be possible to untangle fashion from its ties with biodiversity loss, pollution, the extraction of non-renewable resources on a finite planet and of course the unnecessary waste it creates.

Inspired by nature, some of these new materials are coming out of laboratories right now. It's an incredibly exciting time for new fabric discoveries and who knows, in a few years' time we might all be wearing clothes made from leftover food.

LAB-GROWN SILK

Traditionally silk comes from the cocoons of silk worms. It takes around 1,500 silk worms to produce one metre of silk. But by studying the silk protein that spiders make to spin their webs, biotechnologists have been able to replicate this luxurious fabric by fermenting a mix of yeast, sugar and DNA.

There are up to 8,000 chemicals in a single piece of clothing!

ORANGE PEEL

Chemicals are now being used to extract cellulose from leftover orange rinds to produce a fabric that has the feel of silk.

PINEAPPLE-LEAF FIBRES

Piñatex is made from pineapple-leaf fibres which are a by-product of the pineapple harvest. This waste would normally rot in the ground, but instead it can be turned into biodegradable fabric with similar properties to canvas or leather (without involving chemical-intensive tanneries).

BANANA STEMS

A natural by-product of the food industry, around a billion tonnes of banana stems are wasted each year. Banana-stem fabric has been likened to bamboo and hemp because of its soft texture.

MYCELIUM

Mushroom roots have been used to experiment with new fabrics that use little water, and are biodegradable and non-toxic.

CIRCULAR FASHION

Those working to improve the fashion industry are all talking about circular fashion. It simply means that the materials that are in our clothes are recovered and turned back into new clothes. This would solve lots of problems. It would mean that there would be no new raw materials needed to make our clothes and it would mean there would be no waste. So why are we not doing this already?

The technology to close the loop isn't quite there yet. There have been attempts to make 100 per cent polyester circular so that the fabric can go from garment back to raw materials into a new garment times infinity. However, a lot of materials are made out of mixed fibres so if polyester is mixed with cotton it becomes much more difficult to separate it. This closed-loop approach doesn't work well with natural fibres either because the fibres are weakened. This means recycled natural fibres need to be mixed with new virgin materials to make the new garments strong and wearable.

Fashion designers must factor circularity into how they design clothes if it's to work. It might help designers to think twice about their choice of fabric and steer away from mixed fibres. They should also be thinking about design features down to the fastenings, labels and even the thread (a lot of thread is polyester), which might make it tricky to close the loop. Currently, one per cent of our clothes are recycled into new clothes so there's still a long way to go, but this could have a huge impact in the long-term.

Industry experts have identified 16 key principles
for designers, manufacturers and consumers to use
in order to support and promote circular fashion.

THE 16 KEY PRINCIPLES

1. *Design with a purpose*
2. *Design for longevity*
3. *Design for resource efficiency*
4. *Design for biodegradability*
5. *Design for recyclability*
6. *Source and produce more locally*
7. *Source and produce without toxicity*
8. *Source and produce with efficiency*
9. *Source and produce with renewables*
10. *Source and produce with good ethics*
11. *Provide services to support long life*
12. *Reuse, recycle or compost all remains*
13. *Collaborate well and widely*
14. *Use, wash and repair with care*
15. *Consider rent, loan, swap, second-hand or redesign instead of buying new*
16. *Buy quality as opposed to quantity*

ELVIS & KRESSE

Q&A: Accessory designers

Elvis & Kresse is a design team that rescues materials which would otherwise go to landfill, transforms them into innovative luxury products such as bags, wallets and belts, and donates 50 per cent of its profits to charity.

Tell me about how Elvis & Kresse began.

The starting point was waste. Kresse arrived in the UK in 2004, and in that same year 100 million tonnes of material went to landfill, just in the UK. After visiting landfill sites, waste-transfer stations and recycling facilities, we had a chance encounter with the London Fire Service and fell in love with their damaged, decommissioned fire hoses. We started the business to save them.

What is the problem with the material used to make fire hoses?

Fire hose was designed to be heat-resistant, waterproof and tough . . . so it does not break down or decompose. When it is too damaged to repair it can't be a fire hose any more, but this doesn't mean that it has to languish in landfill. It still has the same incredible properties and deserves to be cherished.

What motivates you?

The environmental challenges that we all face are our key motivators. There is so much to do!

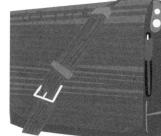

What have been your biggest achievements?

When we set out to solve the problem of the fire hose we had no idea how we would do it, but within five years we had a business that could rescue and transform all of the hoses. It was amazing to have achieved this milestone, and it allowed us to tackle larger problems.

What is a typical day like running your successful brand?

There are no typical days. I (Kresse) might be in the workshop or out with customers or at a landfill site. We could be talking to journalists, making a short film, designing a new product or doing the research on a waste material we are keen to rescue. The only typical thing is a constant effort to balance priorities and make sure we continue to solve waste problems.

What social and environmental impacts have you had?

Since 2005, we have stopped all London fire hoses from going to landfill, and our rescue of 15 different materials has resulted in close to 200 tonnes of material staying out of landfill and remaining in use. We have also donated well over £100,000 to our charitable partners.

What are the future plans for Elvis & Kresse?

We are currently tackling our largest waste challenge: each year 800,000 tonnes of leather offcuts find their way to landfill or incineration. We have created a solution – a way to rescue and reuse all of this material. Fifty per cent of the profits from this rescue are donated to the Barefoot College (an organization that works to set up solar-engineering projects in villages around the world), and in 2019 with Barefoot we created three scholarships for female solar engineers.

DO ZERO WASTE

'Zero waste' in fashion design means designing clothes in a way that cuts out any fabric waste in the production process. Fashion waste falls under two categories: pre-consumer and post-consumer waste. The latter refers to the waste we as consumers create. It's the clothes that we pass on for reusing or recycling – or throw in the bin (if you haven't read this book!).

The other category – pre-consumer waste – is the waste created in making our clothes before the consumer buys them. There are lots of points in the production process where waste can occur. The wrong type of fabric might be ordered, or too much fabric. A brand might order rolls of fabric that don't turn out to be quite the right shade they had hoped for. Maybe they wanted a blue with the vibrancy of a clear summer's day sky and instead receive rolls of navy fabric unsuitable for their collection. Or a brand or designer may completely change their mind and decide orange is the new purple and that everything purple must be destroyed or discarded.

Zero-waste designs already exist! Think of a Japanese kimono or an Indian sari. Both of these garments are created out of complete rectangular shapes so there is no waste.

Pre-consumer waste can also happen because of a fault in the manufacturing process. Sometimes thousands of products in the same batch all have the same problem. Perhaps all the zips don't work on a batch of thousands of jeans, or the seams are unravelling on a batch of shirts which slipped through quality control. That's a lot of waste!

In 2018, high-end fashion brand Burberry admitted to burning £30 million worth of clothes, accessories and perfume instead of selling them off cheaply. They said they had reused the energy from the burning, but they did it in order to protect the brand's exclusivity and value. This made environmental campaigners call for more regulation on waste in the fashion industry.

At Copenhagen Fashion Summit in 2017, the Global Fashion Agenda called on the fashion industry to take action on waste by signing the 2020 Circular Fashion System Commitment. There were four immediate action points including increasing the use of recycled material. In 2019, the French government proposed a ban on the destruction of unsold consumer goods which could be made law by 2023. They estimated that over £625 million worth of goods are thrown away or destroyed in France each year.

IT'S ESTIMATED THAT 15 PER CENT OF ALL FABRIC ENDS UP ON THE FACTORY FLOOR AS WASTE – SWEPT UP INTO BINS AND THROWN AWAY.

Clothes are made out of lots of different shapes: triangles, rectangles, squares, circles, curved shapes of all different sizes and angles. Imagine placing all these shapes on to a rectangular roll of fabric, like a jigsaw with lots of seemingly random and mismatched shapes (this is called 'nesting' by pattern cutters). Depending on how the pieces are cut out of the roll, there are always bits left over. All those bits add up to yet more pre-consumer waste.

The Zero-Waste Design Challenge

Zero-waste designers turn traditional pattern-cutting on its head to create a waste-free zone, which is also more cost-efficient. They adapt the standard traditional block patterns (the building blocks for all garments) so they fit perfectly like a jigsaw on a roll of fabric without the leftover spaces and shapes. Like traditional pattern cutting, zero waste requires an understanding of mathematics and geometry to finely tune a pattern to fit not only the human body but also a roll of fabric. These ideas are an introduction to zero-waste pattern-cutting for you to play around with. Try them with paper first.

T-shirt

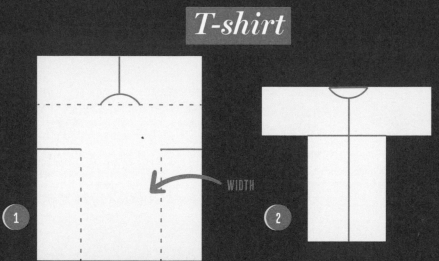

Use an existing T-shirt as a guideline for the width of your T-shirt.

1) Cut along the solid lines in diagram 1.

2) Bring sides of fabric together following dotted fold line into centre of the T-shirt. Stitch seam together to form main body.

3) Bring top of fabric down along the dotted fold line to create the top of the T-shirt and sleeves. Stitch along the edge of the fabric to create sleeves and attach top of T-shirt to main body (seams are shown in diagram 2).

4) Tuck the neck (semi-circle) inside the T-shirt and stitch in place.

Skirt

1) Cut along the solid lines to form four pieces. The smallest widths equal your waist measurement divided by four.

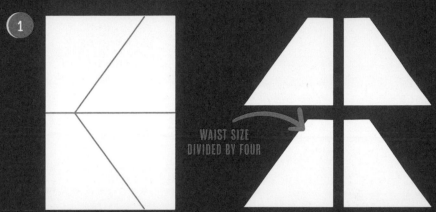

WAIST SIZE
DIVIDED BY FOUR

2) Match the two front and two back pieces. Stitch along the centre to join them together.

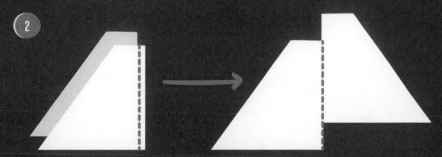

3) Stitch the long sides of front and back together. You can add elastic around the waist and fold into a waistband, or insert a zip at the centre back or side seam. You could add a hem or leave the edge of the fabric raw.

CAN TECHNOLOGY SAVE US?

One of the biggest roles of a designer is to come up with solutions. Phone battery dead? What if your clothes could charge your phone whilst you walk? Increasing levels of air pollution in the city? What if your clothes could convert air pollution into clean air? Growing out of your clothes quickly? How about your clothes grow with you? These are all ways that fashion could be used to make a positive impact.

It's early days for wearable tech, but it has the potential to help those less able-bodied to carry out tasks they may not otherwise be able to do. It could even help people that have health problems be diagnosed or alerted to possible risks. But combining technology with fashion could pose problems in itself. If the technology fails will it be fixable if it's woven into the fabric, and will it be even harder to recycle?

Smart Fashion

The Apple watch was launched in 2015 and quickly became the bestselling wearable device. More recently, Levi's and Google have collaborated to create a denim jacket that connects to your smartphone via Bluetooth, allowing you to control music volume or get directions. Under Armour have created a range of sportswear and bedlinen that absorbs body heat and reflects it back on to the skin as infrared light to aid muscle recovery and relaxation.

Some companies are trying to understand how technology can be used to help trace our clothes from fibre to finished garment through sophisticated tracking systems. It could be used to help fashion brands piece together the journey of their products so that they can confidently know who made their clothes and monitor their supply chains more efficiently and effectively.

It can prove inconvenient when something we've bought online arrives and doesn't fit. Three-dimensional body scanners could eliminate this online-shopping frustration by allowing us to try on clothes in virtual changing rooms before buying. Some believe that in the future, we might all own 3D printers and be downloading our clothes to 3D-print them in our homes for the ultimate zero-waste garment.

GREENWASHING

Why do a lot of fashion brands not know where their clothes come from? The web of supply chains that make our clothes are vast and complicated and they often span continents. Factories may take on orders that are then outsourced to other factories or to homeworkers, making it harder for fashion brands to trace their products as easily. All of these processes require close monitoring.

A company needs to be accountable to others to ensure they uphold standards, and not standards that they have set for themselves. Accountability requires external involvement and collaboration from others, such as government legislation, campaign groups, NGOs, trade unions, workers and us, as citizens, to achieve transparency.

Beware of big statements . . .

It's easy to suffer sustainability fatigue. It can also be incredibly confusing to understand different labelling, to get lost in a brand's annual corporate social-responsibility report or be convinced by a company's marketing spiel. Something may be labelled in a shop as organic but may only have a small fraction of organic material in it without the right certifications. A brand might use recycled paper bags, or liberally use the words 'eco', 'sustainably sourced' or 'environmentally aware' and present themselves as doing the right thing for the planet.

Greenwashing is the term used to describe companies that promote green and ethical practices but don't actually deliver them. They use jargon, or empty words. They may explain their values and beliefs and how much they care for the planet. They may even make commitments for the future and how they're going to make big improvements, but omit telling us how they will carry these out in practice. It might seem impressive to the untrained eye but being aware of greenwashing is your first step to getting closer to the truth.

How to Spot a Greenwasher

Here are some greenwashing red flags to look out for.
Ask the right questions and get the answers you need . . .

'We're energy efficient'

Quite simply a company could be turning off the light bulbs in their shops every day to claim they're energy efficient. They are also required by law in certain countries to use energy-efficient lighting. Is this enough when huge amounts of energy are required to produce clothes?

'Our branding is green'

We associate green with being kind to the planet. This might be misleading. Investigate what the company is doing to reduce their impact on the planet.

'We're reducing our carbon emissions'

It's not enough to fill the offices with plants or install solar panels. Fashion production accounts for 70 per cent of its carbon emissions so this is the area that requires the deepest investigation.

'We have a clothes recycling scheme'

Beware incentives from brands asking you to give them your old clothes for recycling by offering you vouchers. Any good done by recycling is undone by more consumption. Remember less than one per cent of recycled clothes are currently turned into new clothes.

'All our products are sustainable'

Check to see if this applies to one 'special' range or all of a company's products.

'We recycle our packaging'

Again, this could be a way of deflecting attention away from the rest of the production process which is far more damaging to the planet than just the packaging at the end.

'We aim to reduce our carbon emissions by 50 per cent by 2025 . . .'

They may be using a start date in the past when the company output was much smaller. They could also simply express the reduction as a percentage of their output and then increase their output! Who will hold them to account when the end date comes around?

'We give a percentage of our profits to charity'

Donating a percentage of profit from each sale to charity could be seen as an admirable thing to do. So long as we buy the product. Could they donate money to charity without producing the product? Can the brand guarantee that there was no exploitation of anyone involved in the manufacturing of the product, or impact on the environment?

'We're moving towards zero waste'

This could easily be claimed by a company that has only just started to recycle paper in their offices. Is this enough? Delve deeper and find out how zero waste is being achieved.

LOOK OUT FOR A FAIRTRADE LOGO. THIS MEANS A COMPANY IS PAYING A LIVING WAGE TO PEOPLE WORKING IN AT LEAST PART OF ITS SUPPLY CHAIN.

LOOK AT THE SCIENCE THAT COMPANIES ARE BASING TARGETS ON TO REDUCE THEIR IMPACT. ARE THEY BEING REGULATED BY OFFICIAL INDEPENDENT BODIES?

RANA PLAZA

On the 24th April 2013 in Dhaka, Bangladesh, one of the worst industrial disasters ever revealed the harsh and hidden world of fast fashion. The eight-storey Rana Plaza building had been evacuated because cracks had appeared in the concrete floors, walls and ceilings the day before. This huge complex was filled with all sorts of workers, but it was only those in the fashion industry that were told by their bosses that they had to go back into the building to work . . .

The garment workers were not part of a trade union that would have demanded that the building be classified as safe. Furthermore, the threat of losing a month's wages was too much for most. With little choice in the matter, the workers reluctantly entered the building, and it collapsed, killing 1,138 workers and injuring 2,500 others.

Amongst the rubble, bodies lay alongside familiar Western retailer clothes and labels. A lot of brands couldn't confidently say that their clothes weren't being made in a place that had such little regard for human life. Primark was quick to react and donated money to the fund for the families who had tragically lost their loved ones. Despite being associated with Rana Plaza, a few months later Primark reported a rise in profit.

In response to a tragedy like this, some would say that we have no choice but to boycott the brands that feed the problem. Other ethical fashion campaigners, such as the Clean Clothes Campaign, do not condone boycotting brands because it is the people that are working at the bottom of the supply chain, such as the garment workers, that would suffer and likely lose their jobs.

TRIANGLE TRAGEDY

In 1911, a fire at the Triangle Shirtwaist factory in New York killed 146 garment workers, and the Tazreen factory fire in 2012 in Bangladesh killed at least 117 people. Sadly this is not uncommon in Bangladesh as many more factory fires go unreported.

Why is it that garment workers continue to be forced to work in conditions that breach health and safety regulations? And who is responsible for this exploitation? Is it the factory owner who makes his employees work long hours for low pay in unsafe conditions? Is it the local government's responsibility to pass legislation to ensure their citizens have the human right to work with dignity and without risk of injury or death? Is it the fashion brands demanding that the factories produce faster and cheaper goods whilst still maintaining a profit?

Or is it us, by consuming and disposing of our clothes with so little regard for human life? It's clear we all have a part to play, and it's together that we can demand change.

LET'S START A REVOLUTION!

As a response to the Rana Plaza factory collapse, UK designer Carry Somers decided that there needed to be greater transparency in the fashion industry so that brands and retailers could be held to account. Alongside co-founder Orsola de Castro, she founded a global campaign called Fashion Revolution that galvanized the power of people to demand a fairer fashion industry.

Fashion Revolution campaigns for an industry that knows who makes its clothes, from fabric-makers through to the people that sew the garments together. By making companies disclose this information publicly, we can see where they need to improve and find out who are the worst offenders. This can help us to make better decisions as consumers and actively engage with the supply chains that make our clothes. A brand that has nothing to hide should have no problem revealing this information so why do some refuse to?

Fashion Revolution encourages citizens from around the world to ask their favourite brands: 'Who Made My Clothes?'. By utilizing the power of social media, taking to the streets and writing to companies, we show them that we care and show solidarity with the people that make the clothes we wear, often for very little money. With enough pressure we could start to see a more sustainable and ethical fashion industry and the end to tragedies, such as Rana Plaza.

To keep production costs low and profits high, some companies will move to factories and countries where they are guaranteed the cheapest labour.

Why Are Trade Unions Important?

Trade unions are membership bodies that you can join as part of the industry (or trade) you work in. Being a part of a trade union means that if you have a problem at work you can get advice, support and help resolving work-related issues. If there is still a problem, or if it affects a number of others, the union may suggest going on strike to send a clear signal to bosses that this mistreatment will not be tolerated. With the help and support of trade unions in different countries over the years, garment workers have successfully seen an increase in wages, sick-, holiday- and maternity-pay and better working conditions. Sadly, in some countries the power of trade unions has been eroded. It is not uncommon for some employers to see an employee that is a member of a trade union as a potential troublemaker and to intimidate them so they do not make a complaint or even unfairly dismiss them.

Did you know that it's estimated that 80% of the global garment workforce is female?

CAROLYN MAIR

Q&A: Fashion Psychology

Professor Carolyn Mair PhD is the founder of psychology.fashion and author of *The Psychology of Fashion* (Routledge, 2018). Here she answers some questions about what our clothes and clothing choices mean.

What important factors do we consider when buying clothes?

This depends on who's buying the clothing. More consumers are now considering how the clothes were made before they decide to buy. Issues of sustainability and ethics are coming to the forefront, and people are beginning to vote with their wallets. Again it's not simply that 'fast fashion' is bad and 'slow fashion' is good. We need to consider the bigger picture: should fashion be accessible to all or should it be elitist? In my opinion, fashion is for everyone and therefore it should be affordable. Anyway, an item's durability is not just a question of price. Cheaper items can last if they are well cared for during laundry and more expensive items can lose their shape and pill. Surprisingly, many relatively expensive fashion items are made in the same factories as fast fashion.

Sustainable practices are important for the planet, so choosing items that come with information about their environmental cost is a good move. Also, finding out about initiatives that brands are taking to address their social responsibilities can help you make good decisions when buying fashion.

'... MANY RELATIVELY EXPENSIVE FASHION ITEMS ARE MADE IN THE SAME FACTORIES AS FAST FASHION.'

Another factor relates to customer service whether online or in-store. Consumers are becoming more demanding and competition is increasing, so brands need to deliver a convenient, seamless, streamlined service or consumers will go elsewhere. Consumers also like personalized service but some are wary of how their data is used. This can be made clear on the brand's website.

Why do we buy things we don't need?

We are constantly bombarded with fashion imagery showing us how clothes can be our way into a desirable way of life. We are told we need to buy new items to get this lifestyle or achieve success, but it's just not true! Most people don't ever need to buy new clothes, as they already have far more than they wear, but we would get bored wearing the same items forever. We want novelty to stimulate us – meaning we enjoy buying new stuff! The fashion industry is based on this love of novelty.

133

How does the fashion industry make us aspirational?

For a long time, fashion images have shown us a particular ideal which is unrealistic and unattainable for most people. Often, models in these images don't even look like that in real life. There has also been a serious lack of diversity in models, and although this is changing (slowly), there's still a long way to go. Social media has been a double-edged sword. On one hand, it has made fashion more accessible – anyone can be an Instagram influencer and many have done this despite not conforming to the typical fashion ideal.

ARTY?

INTELLIGENT?

ECO-CONSCIOUS?

Bag for Life

WE ARE CONSTANTLY BOMBARDED WITH FASHION IMAGERY.

This is fantastic when it works as it encourages those with unconventional body types to be more confident about their appearance. On the other hand, social media can damage our self-esteem. It's natural to compare ourselves with others, but this can get out of hand online and we judge ourselves too much by the images we see. Even when we know these images have been edited, we are still influenced by them. My advice would be to choose carefully who to follow on social media so that you don't feel worse after checking your feed.

REBELLIOUS?

URBAN?

We judge ourselves too much by the images we see.

WELL TRAVELLED?

SPORTY?

#BE KIND

KIND?

BOHEMIAN?

FEMININE?

FUN?

WEALTHY?

What Do Your Clothes Say About You?

ASK YOURSELF THE FOLLOWING QUESTIONS BEFORE YOU NEXT GO SHOPPING:

- What do you think about when you choose the clothes you wear?

- What are the most important and the least important factors in order?

- How do you feel when you go shopping?

- Do you feel pressure from social media to look a certain way or buy a certain item?

- What might be the reasons why you have bought something and never worn it? How could you avoid a misguided purchase in the future?

- How do the clothes in your wardrobe reflect the person that you want to present to the world?

- Do you know the environmental cost of any of your clothes?

- How much do you know about the sustainability policy of the brands you've bought?

BE THE CHANGE

Q&A: Meet the Experts

Three leading sustainability experts offer their advice to anyone wanting a career in fashion and for anyone wanting to be the change they want to see within the industry.

DR AMY TWIGGER HOLROYD

Associate Professor of Fashion and Sustainability at Nottingham Trent University.

TANSY HOSKINS

Journalist and campaigner, author of *Stitched Up: The Anti-Capitalist Book of Fashion*.

AUDREY DELAPLAGNE

Works in ethical sourcing for global fashion e-tailer ASOS.

What advice would you give someone wanting to work in fashion?

AMY: Be absolutely aware that how the fashion industry is now isn't how it has to be – what seems normal and even 'natural' now must, and will, change. The industry needs people who can dream up new ways of 'doing' fashion that are focused on use, rather than shopping. Could this be you?

TANSY: Most jobs within the fashion industry are harmful to the planet, involve continuing business as usual and hiding the reality of what is produced . . . the science and technology of repair and recycling fashion are exceptions, as is becoming a campaigner for environmental and social justice within fashion or a critical investigative journalist. That is the exciting work that is urgently needed.

Should you work in fashion if you have ethical concerns?

TANSY: Develop a strong moral code for yourself and be prepared to say no and walk away from the industry if you are asked to do immoral things – for example contracting to an unsafe factory, squeezing factories to pay them less, or ordering and using materials that are environmentally hazardous.

AMY: Fashion is bigger than what we tend to think of as the fashion industry: the brands, the shops, the shows . . . you could use design skills to support the reuse and sharing of garments, help people to develop their skills in styling and making, or become an expert in farming sustainable fibres.

AUDREY: The industry needs you . . . There will be days when you will feel like giving up, but remember you are the change, and you are part of a powerful movement that is transforming the industry.

You want to be the change, but how do you do it?

TANSY: The best hope for changing the industry at the moment is for governments to pass laws to protect the planet and to protect workers. This is a job that is well worth working towards – you can do it by exposing wrongdoing and building public support as a campaigner or as a journalist.

AUDREY: One of my mentors said, 'The world is in need of people who are caring, people who are political, people who ask why, and people who use their voice on behalf of those who can't. So when you can, take action, speak up or just bear witness.'

AMY: There is great value in starting the conversation. Knowledge, combined with an activist's drive for change, is incredibly valuable.

MOSES POWERS

Q&A: Catwalk Producer

 Moses Powers is art director and producer of Shangri-La at Glastonbury Festival. He has produced fashion shows for almost 20 years as well as handling international casting and backstage management. Here's his story . . .

What was your journey into this career?

Whilst studying fashion-styling and photography at the London College of Fashion, I met my teacher, Clive Warwick. Working with him on backstage management, I slowly got involved in all other aspects of fashion production. This experience led me to producing and casting for Kokon To Zai for many years.

Tell us a little about what you do and the types of catwalk shows you work on.

I'm lucky enough to have had roles in all aspects of fashion and production from styling to casting and set design. I've worked for small independent designers and agencies working with designers such as Vivienne Westwood, Ashish, Paul Smith, Versace, Julien Macdonald, Nicopanda and many more. My position varies from job to job and depends on the client's needs. My main job now is art directing and producing live events.

What keeps you motivated?

Making the world a better place, working on projects that I feel passionate about and changing the industry to be less wasteful and more conscious. There's no need for the amount of wasted materials and energy spent on short events. Being conscious of this keeps me motivated to be the change I want to see in the industry. My proudest moment is creating a whole set from only recycled and repurposed materials.

What do you like most and least about your job?

Bringing people together to create something unique and amazing is the best. I love using the fashion show as a platform to convey a strong political message to the masses, too. This is why I love working with Ashish and admire what Vivienne Westwood does with her shows, production and climate revolution campaigns. I love fashion as an art form but feel it needs to stop selling a lifestyle that cannot exist. I don't like the waste and fashion's limited ideas of beauty! These two things desperately need to change within the fashion industry. I feel it can be achieved with a conscious effort!

What tips would you give someone looking to break in to fashion show production?

Tip 1: Start by assisting someone you like. I started with an internship. Look for paid internships or apprenticeships.

Tip 2: Try all aspects of the job if you can. That way you gain an understanding of the elements that make up a catwalk show.

Tip 3: Once you've got experience, find a great agency to work for who are producing shows you would really like to work on.

Tip 4: Treat everyone with respect and stay super organized.

Make a FASHION STATEMENT

Fashion is a great way to spread a message. Designers have been using clothes as a vehicle to make big bold statements about social and political issues for decades. Take a look at these legendary fashion activists and be inspired to take part in your own fashion revolution.

DEMNA GVASALIA

At Paris Fashion Week 2019 for Balenciaga, Georgia designer Demna Gvasalia featured European Union imagery and replicas of French rail network uniform to support the workers who were protesting over pension reform. At the same event in 2020, he filled the catwalk with 25cm of water to protest against climate change.

KATHARINE HAMNETT

In 1984, fashion designer Katharine Hamnett met the UK prime minister Margaret Thatcher sporting an anti-nuclear-war slogan T-shirt at 10 Downing Street. She knew that wearing a slogan T-shirt would get media coverage and shine a spotlight on the issue with politicians who could affect change. She continues to create slogan T-shirts today.

VIVIENNE WESTWOOD

Vivienne Westwood uses her catwalk shows and clothing to raise awareness about environmental issues. A fierce climate-change campaigner, critics have said that her views may not be reflected in how sustainable her global fashion business is. But there's no arguing that her work is driven by her passion to change the world. Her motto? Buy less, choose well, make it last.

Inspired to make your own slogan T-shirt? Try block printing an old T. See page 81 for instructions.

START A REVOLUTION

Is there a cause that you care deeply about? Perhaps there's a local issue that needs some attention. A slogan T-shirt on its own might not change the world but partner it with a petition, a demonstration and persuasive letters to change makers, and it is a step in the right direction.

WEAR YOUR VALUES

Your clothing choices matter because everyone's individual actions collectively add up to make a big difference. It's important to remember that we must buy less to truly make a dent in overconsumption and waste. Choosing clothes from brands that are making positive changes to the way they operate is a good start but the amounts that are being produced (and discarded) overall are not sustainable. Now that you've read this book you are armed with the information you need to change the way you consume. Next time you are tempted to go shopping for clothes, remind yourself of our manifesto for an ethical fashion life . . .

DEMAND MORE

Want to know if your favourite brand pays their workers a living wage or what they do with their waste but can't find the answers? Ask them.

STAY INFORMED

As the industry evolves and new problems or solutions are uncovered, keep educating yourself and keep questioning.

GO SECOND-HAND

Use what you have and, if possible, choose second-hand clothes rather than new ones. It's a fun way to experiment with new styles. Pass on your clothes responsibly.

CHOOSE QUALITY

Choose clothes that are made well and will last. Use what you now know about fabrics, and how a garment is finished. Watch out for planned obsolescence.

MAKE DO AND MEND

Care for your clothes and repair them to keep them working for you for longer.

SPREAD THE KNOWLEDGE

Awaken the curiosity of others by talking to friends and using your social-media networks. Have a discussion and listen to opinions and concerns. People don't like being told what they should and shouldn't do without a deeper understanding of the bigger picture.

DISCONNECT TO RECONNECT

Know that the clothes you buy are from nature. We can be inspired by nature by slowing down and reconnecting with our environment. Try unsubscribing from email newsletters that encourage you to go shopping. Switch off from technology from time to time. Follow only those that have a positive influence and are not constantly encouraging you to buy things you don't need.

QUESTION EVERYTHING

Call out greenwashing! Question fashion brands and their policies, practices and commitments. Ask how a brand can claim to be sustainable and still produce so much. (Clue: it can't!) Be critical and don't be fooled by eco buzzwords or nature photographs.

WEAR IT OUT

Wear your clothes, love them and have fun in them! No one cares how many times you wear something – you have found a piece of clothing that is your style, and it deserves to be worn again and again.

AND REMEMBER

. . . IT'S NOT A BARGAIN IF YOU DON'T NEED IT!

What would life be like if we weren't buying lots of stuff? Could we find happiness from having less and doing other things instead? Absolutely!

FASHION EVOLUTION

Fashion is known for evolving and changing but the industry itself, and the way that clothing is produced, has not changed a great deal over the last 300 years. What can we learn from the past in order to end the exploitation of people and the planet in the supply chains that make our clothes?

The mass production of clothes in the 18th century, with its new technologies and streamlined production processes, is responsible for many of the ethical problems we face today. The world of fashion is built on historical systems of exploitation and the plight of the garment workers for better pay and better working conditions that continue to this day.

1600s

Cotton becomes the most popular textile in the world, as cotton garment production in India explodes.

1700s

As new technologies appear in the European Industrial Revolution, new garment factories appear. In 1750, the UK bans the imports of Indian, Persian and Chinese cotton and silk fabrics in order to protect its own industry.

In 1764, James Hargreaves invents the spinning jenny, increasing the speed that yarn can be produced. Indian cloth is replaced by UK-milled cloth across the British Empire. In 1775, £5 million worth of raw cotton is imported to Britain from slave plantations in the Americas.

1800s

The 1800s in Europe and the US see a growth in steam power and iron production, leading to another boom in the creation of new machinery and technology for the clothing and textile industry. In 1804, Dr Cartwright invents the power loom. Homeworkers can no longer compete. There is a rise in slums as workers move to industrialized towns for employment in factories.

Around 1850, commercial sewing machines are developed. In Britain and France, tailors and weavers storm factories, wrecking machinery in protest of their lost livelihoods.

The 1833 the UK Factory Act highlights the number of children under ten working in factories.

The term 'sweatshop' is thought to have been first used in the 1850s to describe factories where workers are treated poorly. This could mean low wages, long working hours, abuse and an unsafe and unsanitary working environment.

1900s

In 1909, with the support of the trade union, 15,000 garment workers go on strike in New York, US, in a battle for better wages and working conditions. It is successful and it initiates a wave of strikes across the country.

In 1911, the Triangle Shirtwaist factory fire in New York kills 146 workers. According to reports, the doors were locked and 62 girls jumped to their deaths, some holding hands. The two youngest of the dead were aged 14. The disaster leads to new workplace safety and labour regulations in the US.

In 1921, the leader of the independence movement against British colonial rule in India, Mahatma Gandhi, calls for a boycott of British cotton textiles. He encourages people to spin their own cotton or buy locally made fabrics. Within four years of the boycott, many UK mills close and thousands of mill workers lose their jobs.

2000s THE RISE OF FAST FASHION

The Spanish high-street retailer Zara is thought to be the pioneer of 'fast fashion' boasting as little as 15 days to get clothes from design to shop floor.

In 2009 in Haiti, garment factory owners (with the help of a US agency) block the Haitian parliament from passing a law to raise the minimum wage.

In 2012, the Tazreen fire in Bangladesh kills at least 117 people. It's reported that the factory fire-exit doors were locked and metal bars were on the windows, trapping workers inside.

In 2013, the Rana Plaza factory collapses in Bangladesh killing 1,138 and injuring 2,500 others.

The International Labour Organization estimates that there are at least 170 million in child labour. Many of these children work

In 1970, the mass production of garments moves to other parts of Asia, particularly Taiwan, South Korea and Hong Kong. Garment workers begin to assert their rights to better pay so some companies move garment production to neighbouring Asian countries, Central America and Mexico in search of a cheaper workforce.

In 1974, the Multi Fibre Agreement is introduced to regulate global trade in the garment industry and impose export quotas on lower economically developed countries.

Between 1985 and 1990, garment production increases in the Philippines, Malaysia, India, Thailand and Indonesia.

A 1991 report reveals that Nike trainers are being produced in an Indonesian 'sweatshop' with poor working conditions and paying workers very low wages.

in the supply chains making our clothes when they should be in school getting an education.

In 2019, thousands of Bangladeshi garment workers protest over low wages and police fire water cannon and tear gas to control the crowds.

In 2019, reports suggest big brands are moving garment manufacturing to Ethiopia as labour, raw material and tax costs rise in Asia. In Ethiopia there is no minimum wage.

In 2019, during London Fashion Week, Extinction Rebellion demonstrators protest against the effect of the fashion industry on climate change.

USEFUL WEBSITES

The fashion industry is changing quickly so make sure you stay on top of ethical developments by checking out these websites:

Anti-Slavery International: **antislavery.org**

Ellen MacArthur Foundation: **www.ellenmacarthurfoundation.org**

Fashion Conscious: **fashion-conscious.org**

Fashion for Good: **fashionforgood.com**

IndustriALL Global Union: **industriall-union.org**

Slow Factory: **slowfactory.global**

UN Fashion Alliance: **unfashionalliance.org**

Labour Behind the Label: **labourbehindthelabel.org**

Clean Clothes Campaign: **cleanclothes.org**

Fashion Revolution: **www.fashionrevolution.org**

United Students Against Sweatshops: **usas.org**

Fairtrade Foundation: **www.fairtrade.org.uk**

Centre for Sustainable Fashion: **sustainable-fashion.com**
Centre for Circular Design: **www.circulardesign.org.uk/research**
C&A Foundation: **www.candafoundation.org**
Soil Association: **www.soilassociation.org**
Pesticide Action Network: **www.pan-uk.org**
Transition Network: **transitionnetwork.org**
Friends of the Earth: **friendsoftheearth.uk**
WRAP: **wrap.org.uk**
World Fair Trade Organization: **wfto.com**

PODCASTS

Wardrobe Crisis **by Clare Press**
Conscious Chatter **by Kestral Jenkins**
Pre-loved Podcast **by Emily Stochl**

WHERE TO FIX YOUR CLOTHES AROUND THE WORLD

Repair Café International: **repaircafe.org**
Fix Ed: **fixing.education**
Restart Project: **therestartproject.org**

WHERE TO SELL YOUR CLOTHES ONLINE

Depop: **www.depop.com**
Ebay: **www.ebay.com**
Etsy: **www.etsy.com/uk**
Thredup: **www.thredup.com**
Vestiaire: **www.vestiairecollective.com**

INDEX

ACKNOWLEDGEMENTS

This book has been a labour of love, benefitting from the passion and empathy of others; united by a sense of duty to the future who believe, as I do, that critical and creative thinking is urgently needed to tackle the climate emergency.

A big thank you to my mentor Rose Sinclair and friend Bridget Harvey for many illuminating conversations and much encouragement over the years. To the countless wonderful people that I have had conversations with at my sustainable fashion talks, workshops and repair cafés over the last decade that have shaped my thoughts and ultimately this book. A special mention to Claire Storey, Penn Smith, Jaime Greenly and Rachael Causer for working alongside me at many 'Worn Well' workshops to share sewing skills and unwavering enthusiasm for clothes repair at a grassroots level.

I'm immensely grateful to Tansy Hoskins, Dr Amy Twigger Holroyd, Audrey Delaplagne, Dr Carolyn Mair, Moses Powers, Kresse Wesling, Alice Wilby and Dilys Williams for adding their voices and contributing to this book. A special thank you to the inspiring spoken word artist and activist Potent Whisper – who works tirelessly to campaign for social good – and penned the powerful words 'to change the world with a change of clothes' when we collaborated together on the #secondhandfirst campaign many years ago.

I am grateful to everyone at Egmont, with a special mention to my editor, Lisa Edwards, who has been wonderfully patient and supportive whilst I finished the book in the early months of motherhood. And not forgetting Kim Hankinson's stunning illustrations that bring the book to life

Many thanks to my family and close friends supporting my work in fashion, sustainability and teaching over the years. A special mention to Beverley Klymkiw for nurturing my love for fashion and sewing from a young age, to Hannah Keever for invaluable advice in the early stages of this book, and to Lourdes Keever for her remarkable ability to foresee and offer help before help is needed. A big thank you to my dear friend and wonderful wordsmith Iain Whiteley for his inspiration, big laughs (always), and belief in my work.

A huge thank you is due to Michael who encourages me to keep learning: to not be afraid to ask questions, delve deep and challenge the status quo. Thank you for your overwhelming support: for numerous cups of tea, for countless (delicious) meals and for pushing our newborn daughter (in her third-hand buggy) around the streets of North London when she was struggling to sleep so I could have some time, space and fuel to work on the book. And finally Etta: you've been with me through this entire journey. Thank you for all the cuddles, for filling my heart with love and bringing me so much joy.